MW00783858

EXPLORING THE UNKNOWN

HISTORIC DIARIES OF BRADFORD WASHBURN'S ALASKA/YUKON EXPEDITIONS

*"A remarkable book describing and capturing in photographs some
of nature's great cathedrals . . . his diaries are absolutely captivating."*
— Jim Whittaker, first American to climb Mount Everest,
author of *Jim Whittaker, A Life on the Edge*

*"This book uniquely captures the wonder, the newness, and
the joy of exploration and of doing things never done before . . . "*
— Royal Robbins, mountaineer

*"Brad Washburn has long been one of my heroes. He approached virgin
mountains with the combined vision of an artist, an athlete, and a scientist."*
— Galen Rowell, mountain photographer, author

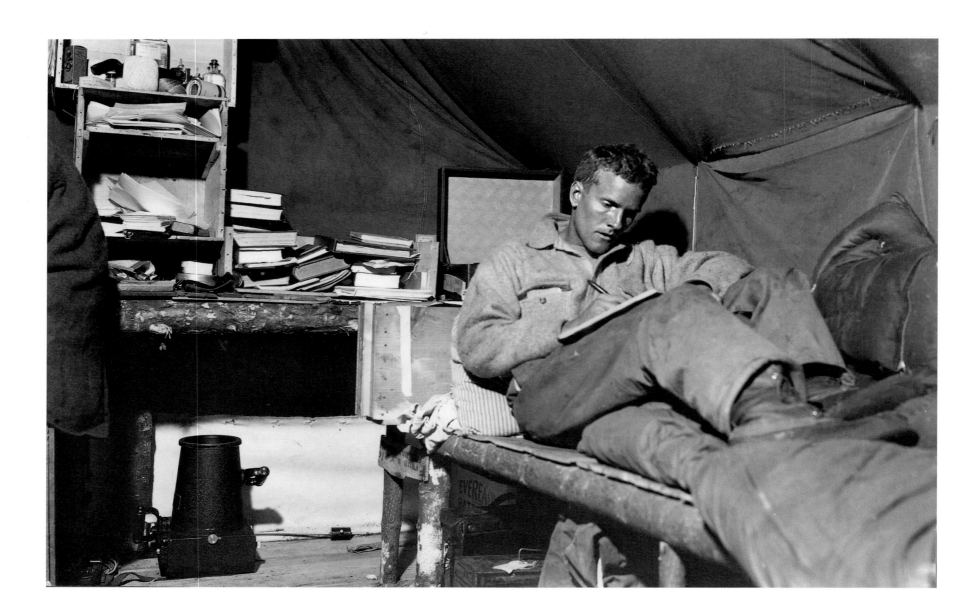

EXPLORING THE UNKNOWN

HISTORIC DIARIES OF BRADFORD WASHBURN'S ALASKA/YUKON EXPEDITIONS

TEXT AND PHOTOGRAPHS BY BRADFORD WASHBURN

EDITED BY LEW FREEDMAN

MOUNT CRILLON

THE YUKON

MOUNT MCKINLEY

EPICENTER PRESS

© 2001 Bradford Washburn

All photographs by Bradford Washburn unless otherwise noted.

All photographs from the Yukon Expedition by Bradford Washburn for the
  National Geographic Society.

No part of this publication may be reproduced, stored in a retrieval system
or on a computer disk, or transmitted, in any form, or by any means,
electronic, mechanical, photocopying, recording, or otherwise without the
prior written permission of the publisher. Permission is given for brief
excerpts to be published with book reviews in newspapers, magazines,
newsletters, and catalogs.

Publisher: Kent Sturgis
Editors: Lew Freedman, Don Graydon
Proofreader: Sherrill Carlson
Designer, production: Jennifer LaRock Shontz

Front cover photographs: *Kahiltna Glacier base camp, Mount McKinley;
  Bradford Washburn on the summit of Mount Bertha.* Photo collage by
  Jennifer LaRock Shontz.
Back cover photographs: *A steep pitch of the Lowell Glacier Icefall.*
  Inset: *Brad Washburn holds his large-format Fairchild F-8 camera.*
Frontispiece: *Bradford Washburn works on his diary inside a tent at the
  expedition's Crillon Lake base camp.*

ISBN 9-945397-92-5 softbound edition

Printed in Canada

First printing March 2001

10 9 8 7 6 5 4 3 2 1

Library of Congress Catalog Card Number: 00 136166

Epicenter Press Inc. is a regional press founded in Alaska whose interests
include but are not limited to the arts, history, environment, and diverse
cultures and lifestyles of the North Pacific and high latitudes. We seek both
the traditional and innovative in publishing nonfiction trade books and gift
books featuring contemporary art and photography.

To order single copies of EXPLORING THE UNKNOWN, mail $19.95
(softbound edition) [Washington residents add sales tax of $1.74] plus
$4.95 for Priority Mail shipping to: Epicenter Press, Box 82368, Kenmore, WA
98028; phone our 24-hour order line, 800-950-6663; or visit our website,
www.EpicenterPress.com

Booksellers: Retail discounts are available from our distributor, Graphic Arts
Center Publishing, Box 10306, Portland, OR 97210. Phone 800-452-3032.

CONTENTS

PREFACE   7

INTRODUCTION   **BRADFORD WASHBURN AND ALASKA**   11

EXPEDITION DIARY I   **THE HARVARD – DARTMOUTH MOUNT CRILLON EXPEDITION** *1934*   19

EXPEDITION DIARY II   **NATIONAL GEOGRAPHIC SOCIETY YUKON EXPEDITION** *1935*   47

EXPEDITION DIARY III   **MOUNT MCKINLEY: FIRST ASCENT OF THE WEST BUTTRESS** *1951*   87

INDEX   127

Aerial photograph of the east face of Mount McKinley's majestic summit pyramid, taken on October 4, 1964.

PREFACE

IT WAS A MOMENT OF BEMUSED REFLECTION during the summer of 1998. Dr. Bradford Washburn and I were standing in Boston's Museum of Science, viewing an exhibit about Mount Everest. At the time he was eighty-eight years old.

Washburn, an esteemed scientist and photographer, mapmaker and mountaineer, was pondering the life he had led—the exciting life he was still living. He was simultaneously sober and lighthearted. His life was really two lives, a portion lived in Boston, Massachusetts, another portion lived in the Alaskan wilderness.

"If I had an obituary in the *Boston Globe,*" Washburn said, "and it was reduced to three or four lines, it would say, 'This man had a vision of Boston's Museum of Science and built it.'"

And in Alaska? I prodded.

"That would be different," he said.

Oh yes. That would be different.

Bradford Washburn is one of the most extraordinary Alaskan figures of all time—despite never living there. In Boston, few picture the museum administrator toting ninety-pound backpacks on his slender frame. In Alaska, few understand his devotion to the museum to which he dedicated virtually all of his professional career.

Two environments, two disciplines, two lives. However, it becomes readily apparent to anyone who spends time with Washburn that those seemingly diverse lives repeatedly intersect in the world of scientific discovery and wonder.

In Alaska today, Bradford Washburn and his wife, Barbara, are admired primarily as pioneering mountaineers, whose achievements in ascents of Mount McKinley, at 20,320 feet the highest peak in North America, are legendary and revered. What is often forgotten is that unlike the modern-day adventurer, most of the couple's accomplishments were recorded in the interests of science.

The adventure, the exploration, and the climb were always inextricably woven into the fabric of the trip. When Washburn planned an expedition to Alaska, usually to attempt a first ascent of a notable mountain, it was not simply about getting to the top. Yes, that was a goal, but equally imperative was the desire to record observations and technical findings, to make the unknown known. Washburn did not travel to Alaska simply to conquer rugged terrain. He went with the idea of explaining the terrain for others to follow. In most instances, that took the form of mapmaking.

In accord with his meticulous nature and innate wish to record, he kept detailed diaries of his Alaska trips, which often spilled over into Canada's neighboring Yukon Territory. As befits his style, Washburn wrote in a basic, straightforward way, with little flowery description. He was, after all, a scientist, not a novelist.

Nonetheless, Washburn's observations, the tales of his trips, the information revealed, are marvelous slices of expedition life from a time before Alaska became a state, from a time before all of Alaska had yet even been seen from an airplane. In many cases, the diaries were used as the basis for the articles Washburn later wrote for the *National Geographic Magazine* and other publications.

Eventually, Bradford and Barbara Washburn donated their papers, diaries included, to the Rasmuson Library Archives at the University of Alaska Fairbanks. Washburn had a close personal relationship with Dr. Terris Moore, a one-time president of the University of Alaska Fairbanks and once a bush pilot who aided Washburn on some critical Alaska missions.

At first the diaries were open to the public. Later, the Washburns chose to seal them from casual perusal until after their deaths. They were available for inspection only with their permission.

I got to know the Washburns through my work as sports editor of the *Anchorage Daily News* in Alaska. I used them as sources for newspaper articles, interviewing them about historical aspects of Mount McKinley or developments related to the mountain. Periodically I wrote feature articles examining some of Bradford Washburn's great climbs or taking note of special anniversaries like those of Barbara Washburn's 1947 McKinley ascent, first by a woman. I was also originally from Boston, and thus over the years our paths crossed frequently not only in Alaska, but also in Massachusetts.

A few years ago, I was granted approval to examine archival material in Fairbanks. The Rasmuson Library, one of the state's great repositories of Alaskan history, contained box after box of material shipped north by the Washburns. I delved into the piles and was rewarded with a delightful experience. Reading and digesting as much as I possibly could in a short time, I examined the Washburn diaries. As a student of Alaska history, and a devotee of mountaineering, I was enthralled. What great adventures. What mesmerizing stories. This was history as it actually occurred. This was the unknown in the process of evolving into the known.

It dawned on me just how privileged I was. Since the diaries had been under lock and key for years, and the adventures themselves had receded from the limelight with the passage of time, I was one of the few living souls with the opportunity to read these documents. It seemed a worthwhile project to bring these stories to light for modern audiences so they can understand what it was like to explore some of Alaska's remote areas for the first time.

The diaries in this book cover three of Washburn's most significant expeditions: his 1934 first ascent of Mount Crillon, then the highest unclimbed peak in the Fairweather Range of Southeast Alaska; his 1935 mapping expedition of the Yukon in the area of Mount Hubbard, on the boundary between Canada and Alaska, a pioneering exploration that revealed hitherto unknown mountains and glaciers; and his 1951 first ascent of the West Buttress route on Mount McKinley, now the standard way up the mountain. The text includes extended edited excerpts from the diaries, along with many of the magnificent mountain photos for which Washburn was renowned.

Washburn was a scientist first and foremost, but the teenager who fell in love with the mountains is never far from the surface in these diaries. In his awe at the scenery, at experiencing the mountains up close, at the phenomenal light of sunset and sunrise, it is clear these experiences touched his soul.

—*Lew Freedman*

Aerial view looking southeast from above the Great Gorge of Ruth Glacier on Mount McKinley

From the southeast, Mount McKinley presents a mass of ridges and sub-peaks leading to the summit at 20,320 feet. The Don Sheldon Amphitheater is in the foreground.

BRADFORD WASHBURN AND ALASKA

BRADFORD WASHBURN WAS BORN IN BOSTON on June 7, 1910. As a youth, he was plagued by hay fever. The man who would later thrive at the highest altitudes, in the thinnest air of North America, had difficulty breathing just above sea level.

He soon discovered, though, that the higher he climbed, the better he breathed. Going up mountains was marvelous for his ability to inhale, and it was also fun. A lifelong fascination and enjoyment of mountains was born. Early climbs in the White Mountains of New Hampshire were followed, in his teens, by climbing in the French Alps.

When Washburn went to Europe in 1926, most of his climbing expenses were met by a generous uncle who had made a fortune selling barbed wire for fences to farmers in the West. Washburn climbed with guides, completing ascents of Mont Blanc, the Matterhorn, and many other peaks. Even then, he had dreams of Alaska. He told his guides that he planned to climb in Alaska, where there were no guides or porters. He insisted that the guides criticize his every move so he would be prepared for Alaska.

Washburn attended the annual meeting of the American Alpine Club in New York in the winter of 1927 and heard mountaineer Allen Carpe talk about his attempt to climb Mount Fairweather in Southeast Alaska. "That is really exciting stuff," Washburn thought at the time.

Little did he know how exciting Alaska would prove to be for him, nor how much it would become a dominant theme in his life. In 1930, Washburn explored the approaches to Mount Fairweather—his first of nearly seventy trips to Alaska or the Yukon, appropriately spanning seventy years.

In 1927, George P. Putnam and Sons published Washburn's first book, *Among the Alps*, as part of a series of mountaineering books written by boys for boys. Putnam later published Washburn's account of climbing New Hampshire's Mount Washington and his first book related to Alaska, *Bradford on Mount Fairweather*. Royalties from the books helped pay for Washburn's education while he was still in high school and later at Harvard.

In the years that followed, Washburn put together the most intriguing Alaska climbing resume of all time, even if he was born too late to make the first ascent of Mount McKinley. During the first thirteen years of the twentieth century, a handful of mountaineering parties made notable assaults on the peak. McKinley was first climbed in 1913 by an expedition led by Hudson Stuck, the Episcopal archdeacon of the Yukon. The first man to set foot on the summit was one of Stuck's partners, Walter Harper, an Athabascan Indian from Interior Alaska. The date was June 7, 1913—Brad Washburn's third birthday.

Stuck, incidentally, was a firm proponent of the use of the Native name for the mountain—Denali, meaning "the high one" or "the great one"—rather than Mount McKinley, named in 1896 for William McKinley, then the Republican nominee for president of the United States. McKinley was the name in most common use at the time of Washburn's expeditions, and it is the name used in this book. However, Denali has won wide acceptance, even though the official name remains McKinley.

Once the summit prize was claimed, interest diminished in future McKinley climbs. World War I intervened, and then the Great Depression ruled the American economy. Mountaineering for much of the century was about first ascents. If something had been done once, many felt there was no point in doing it again.

Washburn always appreciated being the first to the top of a particular mountain, but it was part of his vision that he could always see beyond the summit. For him, the experience of the climb was important, but studying and understanding the mountain was more important still. At a time in history when going off to the mountains to climb around on snow and ice seemed frivolous to much of the public, Washburn had the intelligence, organization, and talent to attract sponsors, and he had the standing in the scientific community to make his opinions and findings known.

Washburn was twenty-eight when he became director of the New England Museum of Natural History on March 3, 1939. The museum, forerunner of today's Museum of Science, then attracted 44,000 visitors a year. Washburn, who remained director until 1980, jokes that "I worked there for forty-one years without a promotion!"

Washburn never really retired. He retains an office at the museum, and in his ninetieth year still put in full work days as honorary director. In the year 2000, the museum attracted 1.6 million visitors and its budget was close to $40 million.

By the time Washburn ascended to the directorship of the Museum of Science, he had amassed an impressive history of Alaskan climbing and exploration, and he had established an important rapport with the National Geographic Society.

In 1934, Washburn made his inaugural first ascent of a major Alaskan peak, with the first climb of Mount Crillon, a 12,728-foot mountain in Southeast Alaska. The following year he led a three-month surveying expedition, sponsored by the National Geographic Society, into the Canadian Yukon on the border with Alaska.

Washburn's trips always involved exploration, surveying, and photography. Typically he took hundreds of large-format photographs of the areas he visited—not from the ground, but from the air. State-of-the-art aerial photography appealed to him, but state-of-the-art at the time was a risky proposition. Washburn's daring style meant removing the door of a small, unpressurized plane, roping himself firmly into the doorway, and shooting pictures as the plane cruised over the snowbound wilderness.

Washburn and the pilots who took him aloft were sometimes the first humans ever to see an area. It is humbling to realize in this jet age, when humans have explored outer space and walked on the moon, that as recently as 1935, no aircraft had flown over the entirety of the Seward and Hubbard Glaciers of the Yukon and Alaska until Washburn's flights.

Washburn got his first chance to approach Mount McKinley after Gilbert Grosvenor Sr., president of the National Geographic Society, asked him in 1936 if he knew of any other worthwhile projects in Alaska that would be exciting and not too terribly expensive.

His answer? Fly around Mount McKinley and take pictures with large-format film. Such aerial photographs would add immeasurably to the understanding of the country's most famous peak.

Washburn, who had not yet joined the Museum of Science and was supporting himself as a lecturer and freelance writer, told Grosvenor he could probably do the job for about $1,000. Washburn then persuaded Pan American World Airways to provide a twin-engine Lockheed Electra for the flights, and he had himself a deal.

Washburn strapped himself into one of these planes in flight, with the door removed, and began firing off his camera. The flights emanated from

The southern expanse of Mount McKinley spreads out in a distant view from the Tokositna Valley.

Fairbanks, and at least one hour was spent over McKinley on three separate occasions. When the photo flights were complete, Washburn sent Grosvenor a $35 refund check for the amount left over from the $1,000 advance.

In 1937, Washburn and his friend Bob Bates made the first ascent of Mount Lucania, a 17,150-foot mountain in the St. Elias Range—then the highest unclimbed peak in North America. Their adventure was featured in an eight-page, illustrated article in *Life* magazine. On the same journey they also made the second ascent of nearby 16,600-foot Mount Steele—an ascent required as part of their frantic retreat back to civilization.

In 1938, Washburn led the first ascent of Mount Marcus Baker, at 13,250 feet the tallest mountain in the Chugach Range, which abuts the city of Anchorage. Later that year he added the first ascent of 16,200-foot Mount Sanford to his record, climbing to the top on skis with lifelong friend Terris Moore.

During the summer of 1940, Washburn gained a new climbing partner: his wife. Barbara Washburn had no climbing background when she married Brad in 1940, but soon she found herself a full-fledged team member on expeditions to Alaska.

"It never occurred to me to think I was going to have to come," she said of her husband's Alaska expeditions. "I just thought he was going to marry me, we'd have children and that would be the end of it."

Not quite.

In 1940, Barbara was part of the team that made the first ascent of 10,182-foot Mount Bertha in Southeast Alaska. In 1941, she was a member of the team that made the first ascent of the much more difficult Mount Hayes, a 13,740-foot peak in the Alaska Range.

In the summer of 1942, while World War II raged in Europe and the Pacific, Washburn was assigned to the U.S. Army Alaskan Test Expedition, with the task of testing equipment under frigid conditions. Looking for the most rugged cold-weather environment possible, the group was sent to Mount McKinley. The team of seventeen men spent three months on the mountain, testing radios, tents, sleeping bags, clothing, and food.

The men spent most of their time testing food and gear, but finding themselves at a 17,400-foot camp, they felt they might as well climb to the top. Only two days were devoted solely to the summit climb, but seven men went all the way in beautiful, windless weather. Colonel Marchman, the expedition leader, had radioed from base camp and announced, "Mount McKinley will be climbed today!" Washburn said this was probably the only mountain in history ever to be climbed under U.S. Army orders.

The 1942 climb was only the third ascent ever of McKinley. It was on that climb that Washburn realized the need to prepare a detailed map of the mountain. Because of the limited maps of the day, he said, "A lot of the time we didn't know exactly where we were." In 1960 he published the first definitive map of the mountain, the only primary map still used by the thousand or so climbers who attempt to ascend the peak each spring.

The McKinley map is one of several that established Washburn's prominence in the creation of detailed wilderness maps. Over the course of several years in the 1970s, he and Barbara surveyed the Grand Canyon for a map of that great landscape. In the 1980s, he led the successful effort to carry out aerial mapping of Mount Everest. Both projects were funded by the National Geographic Society.

After World War II, Washburn did not return to Alaska until 1947, when he led a large team that climbed Mount McKinley, again via the original Muldrow Glacier route. On that trip, starting in March, they spent three full months on the peak, and it was at that time that Barbara recorded the first ascent of McKinley by a woman.

Also on this trip, an aerial reconnaissance by Washburn convinced him that the shortest, safest way to climb Mount McKinley was up its "back side"— via the Kahiltna Glacier and the mountain's West Buttress.

The first ascent of the West Buttress route was made in 1951, with Washburn leading a superb eight-man team. The pioneering effort on this route demonstrated that McKinley could be climbed much more readily if climbers were flown in to a high base camp on the Kahiltna Glacier rather than trekking miles and miles over the tundra from the north and then hauling gear all the way up the lengthy Muldrow Glacier.

When Washburn completed his 1951 ascent of Mount McKinley—his third—he was forty-one years old. He and his partner Jim Gale knew instinctively they would not return. On the descent, tears ran down the cheeks of these tough and strong climbers because they knew they had stood on the summit of North America for the last time.

The West Buttress route quickly became the most common path to the summit, and its popularity has led some to offer it little respect, even to calling it a "walk-up." But this is a ludicrous description for a route on which temperatures can drop to minus 40 degrees, winds can blow at 90 mph or more, and storms blow in with little notice—and where even a careful mountaineer may drop into a deadly crevasse, and climbers must make 13,000 feet of vertical gain during their ascent.

Washburn's climb of 9,500-foot Mount Dickey in 1955 marked the last time that he completed a first ascent of an Alaskan peak. He used the summit of Dickey as the final survey point needed to finish the southeast corner of his map of Mount McKinley. Washburn's immersion in McKinley makes it sometimes difficult to separate the man from the mountain. Some even joke that Washburn invented the mountain.

Washburn never wearies of his identification with Mount McKinley. He is proud of his deeds, but gladdest, it seems, to be an educator, a conduit of information about the mountain. He has become a custodian of mountain lore and a generous purveyor of information about the men who went to McKinley in the early years of the twentieth century. Along with his admiration for the early pioneers is his thorough contempt for Frederick Cook, who claimed to have made the first ascent of the mountain.

Cook claimed that he made a round-trip to the summit in twelve days in September 1906 and, for a short while, he was believed. As far back as the 1950s, Washburn and Adams Carter believed their research had put Cook's claim to rest. And even then, Washburn felt he was merely following up on the convincing evidence established by his old friend Belmore Browne.

A fresh generation of Cook backers surfaced in the 1990s, helped by a sizable bequest to the Frederick A. Cook Society from Cook's granddaughter, Janet Vetter of Florida. Washburn was furious that the Cook society renewed attacks on Browne, who with two partners had climbed to within two hundred yards of the summit of McKinley in 1912 before turning back in a terrible gale.

Washburn devoted himself to proving the falsehood of Cook's McKinley claim. He clearly demonstrated through scientific means, including photography and global positioning system surveying, that Cook's alleged picture of the summit was taken from a mountain more than nineteen miles away and barely 5,000 feet high.

In proving the Cook hoax, Washburn was not only protecting the memory of Hudson Stuck and the other members of the 1913 party that first climbed McKinley, but that of Browne and his companions, who came so tantalizingly close to the summit the year before. Browne's story always stuck with Washburn.

"This terrible windstorm hit them with such force that they just couldn't stand up," he said, "and Belmore crawled on his hands and knees until he just couldn't go any farther. He said they could see the summit between the gusts, they knew they were almost there, but simply couldn't move another inch."

The spot, Washburn realized later when he climbed McKinley, was only a dozen easy minutes from the top. In 1947, George Browne, Belmore's son, accompanied Brad and Barbara Washburn on their successful ascent of McKinley.

"When Belmore's son climbed to the top," Brad Washburn said, "he was almost sick when he saw where his father was forced to quit."

Despite the passage of years, Washburn's energy and love of Alaska never seems to flag. He and Barbara continue to make trips north to open exhibits of photographs or give lectures or attend celebrations of notable occasions in mountaineering history. In the spring of 1999, Brad and Barbara were inducted into the newly created Alaska Climbers Hall of Fame in Talkeetna,

Mount McKinley rises above a girdle of billowing clouds. The view is from Stony Hill, on the Muldrow Glacier (northeast) side of the mountain.

the community north of Anchorage that serves as the jumping-off point for pilots and their mountaineer customers who attempt to climb McKinley via the West Buttress.

The induction ceremony was held in the vast lobby of the new Talkeetna Alaskan Lodge—a lobby decorated with climbing pictures and with old gear from Washburn's collection preserved in glass cases. From the hotel's rear deck is an unobstructed view of McKinley—if it's a clear day. On this particular day, the mountain chose to reveal itself, giving the inductees and guests the opportunity to mingle outside and gaze at the incredible breadth and beauty of the peak. Barbara Washburn, then eighty-four, was gaily attired, and with her thick white hair had a distinguished look. Brad Washburn, still retaining an energetic voice and erect bearing, chatted amiably with friends and strangers. A month shy of turning eighty-nine, he joked about his age and jovially called this elderly version of himself "the remnant" of his old, vigorous climbing body.

Late in 1999, when the *Anchorage Daily News* was soliciting votes to choose the top Alaskan athlete of the twentieth century, Washburn made it his business to call me and lobby for Walter Harper, the first person to ever set foot on the summit of Mount McKinley. Taking the trouble to campaign for Harper indicated both the continuing depth of Washburn's passion for the mountain and his admiration for those climbers who came before him.

"The accomplishment of what he did at that time wipes everyone else off the list," Washburn said of Harper. "Those guys did it with no map."

Most of the time, Washburn also did his own Alaska climbs with little in the way of maps. After all, he was the one busy making them.

It is not surprising that mountaineers who wanted to make exceptional climbs in Alaska often found their way to Washburn's door, hoping to receive advice, and a benediction of sorts. Washburn still encourages a younger generation of strong climbers. "Quite a guy," he might say of a mountaineer with big dreams. Of course, if any climbers were foolish enough to leave Washburn with the impression they were ill-prepared for the task ahead, Washburn had no hesitation in warning them away.

For a good portion of the twentieth century, adventurers could find the wildest conceivable country in Alaska. And that was precisely what appealed to sixteen-year-old Bradford Washburn when he attended that American Alpine Club lecture and thrilled to Allen Carpe's description of his first attempt to climb Mount Fairweather. At the same gathering, he listened intently as Osgood Field recounted his experiences at Glacier Bay, Alaska. The most marvelous word pictures lodged in the mind of an eager teen.

"I was absolutely fascinated by the beauty, the midsummer snowstorms, the real wilderness," Washburn said decades later. "These men seemed to have guts unlimited. I simply couldn't wait to go to Alaska."

—*Lew Freedman*

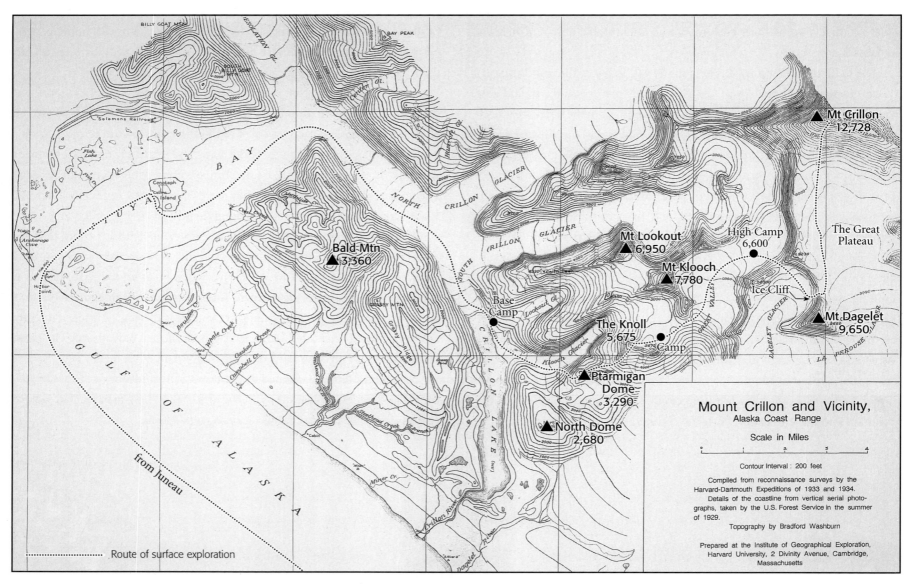

Members of the 1934 expedition flew to Crillon Lake to begin their effort to accomplish the first ascent of Mount Crillon in Alaska's Fairweather Range.
Prepared by Bradford Washburn at the Institute of Geographical Exploration, Harvard University. Reproduction courtesy of National Geographic Society.

THE HARVARD – DARTMOUTH MOUNT CRILLON EXPEDITION 1934

To the members of our 1934 expedition, who toiled valiantly in
order to make possible the first ascent of Mount Crillon.

IN THE SUMMER OF 1934, BRADFORD WASHBURN made his first major ascent of an unclimbed Alaskan peak.

Mount Crillon, a 12,728-foot mountain in Southeast Alaska, beckoned. By then it could be classified as unfinished business. In 1932, a Washburn party reconnoitered the approaches to this huge, unmapped wilderness peak. In 1933 he fielded a strong party that was turned back by bad weather only a trifle below the summit. Food, supplies, and time then ran out as Mount Crillon again proved to be a tougher customer than the climbers had expected.

For the 1934 expedition, an ascent of the mountain was by no means the sole objective. Richard Goldthwait, a young geologist, took ice-depth soundings on South Crillon Glacier, above the expedition's base camp, determining that the glacier was 840 feet thick. It was the first time anyone had successfully measured the ice thickness of an Alaskan glacier. Members of the expedition also measured the speed of the glacier, discovering that it was moving at a rate of up to two inches per hour—and that its movement was significantly faster on clear days than on rainy days.

Washburn's interest in Crillon was something of a by-product of an old desire to climb Mount Fairweather, the great 15,300-foot coastal peak nearby. His very first Alaskan journey, in 1930 when he was barely twenty years old, revolved around exploring that mountain.

"We didn't get anywhere near the top," Washburn said. "We learned how big Alaska is and how big that mountain was."

Fairweather was conquered by other climbers in 1931, but Washburn still considered the summit of Fairweather a worthy prize, by a different route. That goal, too, was thwarted in 1932 when a floatplane transporting supplies to the expedition found no place to land.

Only then did Washburn and his partners turn their attention to Mount Crillon.

"There we were," he said. "So we decided on the second-highest peak in the range."

They returned to Mount Crillon in 1933. And again in 1934.

"We stubbornly went back," Washburn said.

The third time, they reached the summit.

The Harvard-Dartmouth Mount Crillon Expedition of 1934 made the first ascent of the 12,728-foot peak in the Fairweather Range. In the team were (back row, from left) Dave Putnam, Russ Dow, Bob Stix, Bem Woods, Wok Holcombe; (middle row) pilot Gene Meyring, Brad Washburn, Linc Washburn, Hal Kellogg, Dick Goldthwait; (front) Ad Carter and Ted Streeter.

THE HARVARD – DARTMOUTH
MOUNT CRILLON EXPEDITION, 1934

Bradford (Brad) Washburn (leader), of Cambridge, Massachusetts

Adams (Ad) Carter, of Jefferson, New Hampshire

Russell (Russ) Dow, of Woodsville, New Hampshire

Richard P. (Dick) Goldthwait, of Hanover, New Hampshire

Waldo (Wok) Holcombe, of Cambridge, Massachusetts

Howard (Hal) Kellogg, of New York City

David (Dave) Putnam, of Keene, New Hampshire

Robert (Bob) Stix, of Scarsdale, New York

Edward (Ted) Streeter, of Stonington, Connecticut

A. Lincoln (Linc) Washburn, of Hanover, New Hampshire

Henry S. (Bem) Woods, of Hanover, New Hampshire

A year before the first successful ascent of Mount Crillon, another party led by Bradford Washburn found the best route for approaching the summit. In the team were (from left) Charley Houston, Bob Bates, Bill Child, Brad Washburn, Walt Everett, and Ad Carter.

CRILLON LAKE BASE CAMP
FAIRWEATHER RANGE, ALASKA

FRIDAY, JUNE 22, 1934

We had the most wonderfully beautiful plane ride of my life today. Icy Strait was clear, with silvery seas of clouds to the west and north and the whole Fairweather Range rising silhouetted against the pale evening sky. Hal Kellogg thought the mountains were a mirage.

We're in a powerful Lockheed Vega, with pilot Gene Meyring at the controls. We hit a short rain squall off Icy Point and followed the beach, flying low over the breakers. We crossed the La Perouse Glacier exactly one hour out of Juneau, and five minutes later good old Crillon Lake appeared through a tiny rift in the clouds.

We slipped in through a narrow opening between the clouds and treetops and roared down the lake in just two minutes to the South Crillon Glacier. Swinging back after a good survey of the water for icebergs, we cut the motor and glided in a semicircle to a perfect landing between the chunks of floating ice. We taxied to the shore and went ashore and hurriedly dumped our stuff on the bank.

I hopped back into the plane with Gene and the mechanic and we headed a short distance up the coast to Lituya Bay. Bert Maycock's boat, the *Pheasant*, was waiting at the bay, along with four of our men—Dick Goldthwait, Russell Dow, Dave Putnam, and Ad Carter.

We hurriedly loaded the plane with tents, tarps, and sleeping bags, and took off again, flying low and fast above the beaches and back toward Crillon Lake. Unloading at camp took only a few moments, and then Gene made a hasty getaway for the bay in almost pitch darkness. We have a roaring fire going now.

Jim Huscroft lived by himself on Cenotaph Island in Lituya Bay and raised foxes. The climbers visited him on their way to and from Mount Crillon.

What a grand feeling it is to be back here again with the old glacier cracking and the wind singing in the trees and the water lapping on the shore. The thrushes are simply glorious, singing so hard and steadily that they almost keep one from thinking. It's all happened so suddenly I can scarcely believe we've started in on Mount Crillon all over again. We're truly under way with the Harvard-Dartmouth Expedition, which owes its name to the fact that of the eleven men in the party, four (Ad, Wok, Hal, and I) went to Harvard and four (Dick, Linc, Dave, and Bem) went to Dartmouth.

SATURDAY, JUNE 23

I awoke when Gene Meyring's plane came roaring down right over the tent. All the mist was gone. It was seven o'clock and the sun was shining brightly on the icefront. After we unloaded the plane, I flew back to Lituya Bay with Gene and stayed for a breakfast of some of those amazing old sourdough hotcakes made by Jim Huscroft, a hermit who lives on Cenotaph Island in the bay. It seemed like old times. We brought him his Christmas mail.

The next airplane load was the most vital of the whole summer and had us all worrying till we nearly burst. We planned to airdrop supplies to a 5,600-foot-high campsite we called the Knoll—free-fall, with nobody up there.

We loaded the plane just level with thirty-one boxes and tents. The mechanic and I rode in the rear of the Lockheed Vega. The plane was so full that I had to crouch with my knees against my chin and hold a box from falling on top of me as we taxied toward the ocean to take off.

We swung up the bay in a gentle arc, climbed up the Crillon Glacier, over Crillon Lake, and over La Perouse Glacier. My, but Mount Crillon looked enormous in the morning light, its great glittering icefalls and cornices towering far above us as we circled slowly around.

In a moment the crest of the Knoll appeared below us. We had to allow for a terrific drift due to our speed and an altitude of at least 1,000 feet above the Knoll snowfield. The first box went out and sailed gradually downward, turning over and over in the air as it went—for what seemed an interminable time. First it looked as if it would surely fall into a crevasse. Finally after a

Pilot Gene Meyring sits atop his powerful Lockheed Vega seaplane by our Crillon Lake base camp. The expedition air-dropped tents and supply boxes from Gene's plane onto an upper campsite called the Knoll, at 5,600 feet elevation.

ten-second plunge it buried itself safely in the slushy snow and without breaking, exactly where we'd wanted it to fall.

The dumping was a delicate business at best and we were getting a bit reckless. One box got stuck in the door and didn't go out till an instant too late. It sailed downward. At first it looked OK, but then it began to approach dangerously close to the great 3,000-foot cliff that drops from the edge of the Knoll snowfield to the Dagelet Glacier. It just barely missed hitting a pinnacle of rock, completely cleared the snowfield, and hurtled out of sight down a 50-degree snow gully, walled by beetling crags of rock that dropped all the way to the glacier below. The box lodged in a tiny strip of snow, plastered onto the rocks of the east wall of the gully. Would we ever be able to retrieve it from such a spot?

From the air, each box showed up clearly, lying in a little crater it had blown for itself in the soft snow. The boxes were all numbered and painted orange. We had no more close shaves and an hour and twenty minutes after leaving Lituya Bay, we glided down onto the water again just as the *Pheasant* with the last of our fellows aboard was entering the bay. Our plans were clicking like the best watch that ever was made—and to see such a complicated network of intertwining schemes panning out did my heart good.

Back at our Crillon Lake base camp, we spent the afternoon laying the tent floor and the evening in setting up the big tent and its tarp porch. The flies and no-see-ums are certainly vicious this year—the mosquitoes are a bit sluggish and haven't developed a speedy stinging technique yet. The radio is set up already and Dave Putnam has got us some music from Hollywood.

MONDAY, JUNE 25

We got under way at 6:00 a.m. in a couple of groups, to make the 5,000-foot climb up to the Knoll to retrieve the airdropped boxes. The clouds were low, and the walk up Klooch Glacier and over the gravel flats was cool and comfortable. We reached Ptarmigan Dome in two hours and ten minutes, and then came the most lovely walk imaginable, along a ridge which was already all covered with deep heather and lupine.

At Bivouac Rock we came out of the clouds and emerged into a gorgeous, sunlit world above a shimmering sea of clouds stretching as far as the eye could reach in every direction. We climbed on through continually deeper and deeper slush. At Porcupine Gulch we roped up before tackling the rocks of Knoll Ridge. They were snow-covered and corniced in places, but for the time of year were in remarkable condition—much easier than early July a year ago.

By 11:00 a.m. we were atop the west peak of the Knoll, eating lunch in the blazing hot sun and just screaming for lack of water. The air was so still. Crillon rose majestically above us, her summit cornice much larger than last year.

We reached the summit of the Knoll after a forty-minute fight in bottomless slush. Boxes lay everywhere ahead of us, each in a crater about eighteen inches deep. We broke into three groups. Russ Dow, Wok Holcombe, and I climbed to the top of the ridge with my map. Ad Carter and Bem Woods went on skis after two isolated boxes. Hal Kellogg and Linc Washburn (no relation to me) worked on the flat terrain where sixteen pockmarks had been clearly visible from the plane.

Russ and I left for the big gully to try to retrieve the box that had dropped so dramatically into it. I went ahead to investigate, standing tip-toe near a ledge that overlooked the 3,000-foot drop to the Dagelet Glacier. I peeked down the chute and there was the box, just ten feet below me, but I didn't dare go for it without a rope. So we promptly roped up.

Russ belayed me as I picked my way gingerly down the ice. There were no real footholds. I loosened the box with a finger touch—even a breeze would have sent it down the glacier. Then I pushed it up ahead of me while Russ hauled me with the rope.

We tallied up our heaps and found every single thing. Only six or seven cans had been ruined from a box of peas that split open. A worthwhile sacrifice.

TUESDAY, JUNE 26

Here at our base camp at Crillon Lake, everything is beautifully fixed up now, with the radio operating perfectly, the Victrola in place, lots of mosquito

The 190-foot end of South Crillon Glacier towers above Dave Putnam and Wok Holcombe in their tiny canoe at the west end of Crillon Lake.

netting, and a screen door on hinges. Only a few moments ago the radio transmitter worked for the first time. Dave contacted a fellow in Oregon and sent a message home through him. What a marvelous thing this radio is.

THURSDAY, JUNE 28

Up at 2:30 a.m. at the lake and cooked breakfast for Hal, Bem, Linc, Dave, and myself. It was sombre when we left base camp, with slight tinges of pink showing through layers of high clouds in confused masses above the Knoll. All was cool and damp and beautiful as we trudged slowly up the glacier in the gray of dawn, packing nearly sixty-pound loads up to our cache on the Knoll. This trek up more than 5,000 feet in elevation and back in a single day is something.

We again roped up on the approach to Knoll Ridge. A low sea of clouds drifted lazily below us across the ocean, lit here and there by shafts of light that pierced rifts in the upper ceiling. A radio conversation with the base camp went off excellently: We ordered raspberry tarts for supper. We took some movies around the cache and then enjoyed a thirty-minute nap before the return journey to camp.

FRIDAY, JUNE 29

Up at 2:30—awake at least—with a great yell from Wok that the oatmeal was burned. I drifted back to sleep again only to be awakened once more by a pandemonium when Ad put salt on the burned oatmeal instead of sugar.

There was no use trying to sleep anymore, so I played Viennese waltzes on the Victrola until the row ceased and the two of them left for the Knoll with Russ and Ted. At seven o'clock I awoke again when Ted returned because of a sore ankle.

Everyone else returned from the Knoll at 7:00 p.m. after a terribly hot, heavy, slushy trip, simply burned to a frazzle. Ted is not so well tonight. He has a stomachache and a pretty badly infected finger.

SATURDAY, JUNE 30

A cold northeast wind is coming down the lake. Hoping to get up in the air and take photographs, we waited for our plane's scheduled arrival, but no plane appeared. The dependability of airplanes here is between zero and minus one. Instead, Bem and Bob and I went over to the glacier in the canoe and put up a cement pillar on which to place the theodolite, our surveyor's instrument, as a glacier-speed-measuring tool.

Ted is still in lousy shape, and so we are setting up plans for tomorrow as follows: Linc, Russ, and Ad are leaving at 4:00 a.m. for the Knoll with their sleepers and the remaining stuff necessary for actually living up there—salt, cereal, stove, and kitchen.

MONDAY, JULY 2

Huge orgy for supper: three grouse, corn fritters, bran muffins, new potatoes, spinach, fudge. The radio schedule from the three men camped at the Knoll came in beautifully at 7:00 p.m. Ad said they were in a cold northwest wind, with everything freezing over fast. They asked how to keep the Logan tents from flapping. I laughed at that. There's no way I've even been able to discover that will do that.

TUESDAY, JULY 3

Wok, Hal, and Bob left for the Knoll in the morning. I had a radio chat with the Knoll, and the news from there was excellent. Last night there was a howling gale that nearly ripped down the tents—but this resulted in a swell hard crust on which Linc and Russ took three loads each around Klooch Corner, further up the route, and Ad took two loads.

In the afternoon I took two hundred feet of film of Dick's blasting apparatus in operation on the Klooch Glacier, which he's using to get seismic depth readings. Boy, but the dynamite certainly pooped merrily for the pictures.

David Putnam at his radio at Mount Crillon Base Camp in 1934. This radio was of vital importance to the success of this expedition.

Geologist Dick Goldthwait works with seismic sounding apparatus on the South Crillon Glacier, the first time such work had been carried out on an Alaska glacier. He discovered the ice depth to be 840 feet.

WEDNESDAY, JULY 4

Went to take movies of the Crillon Glacier in the beautiful morning light. And what glorious light and shadow it was. The greens and blues and delicate shades and shadows in that cliff of ice are simply astonishing.

We certainly have a swell place for this camp, and it hasn't rained since we've been here. To bed at 10:00 p.m. after the radio schedule with Prince Rupert, British Columbia, with a message for me from the family at last: "Brad—All well—merry 4th of July to you all. All kinds of good luck! Father and Mother."

THURSDAY, JULY 5

Our luck finally ran out on the rain. It was pouring on us when we woke up. We had radio contact with the Knoll at noon, and they had a hard snowstorm going. We had a six o'clock radio schedule, but have had no reply at all. I'm afraid their set is broken.

Just now Dave has blown all the tubes in our radio receiver for some unknown reason. No radio here, no radio at the Knoll, no airplane, and rotten weather.

FRIDAY, JULY 6

Bob and Linc came down from the Knoll with the radio. Their trouble, luckily, was only a broken battery cable. And Dave did a wonderful job fixing our receiver. We packed up Bem and Ted and got them off for the Knoll with the radio and with cereal, sugar, salt, and other goods. Ted seems stronger now.

SATURDAY, JULY 7

We spent the morning working in a gentle drizzle at remeasuring our surveying baseline. We completed this by lunchtime without any more catastrophes. Linc and I then canoed down the lake and hiked up to Reflection Pond to establish its elevation and carry out some exploration and got back to camp in the late afternoon.

The 8:00 a.m., noon, and now the 8:00 p.m. radio schedules with the Knoll yielded nothing at all, and at 8:15 we became worried as to whether Ted and Bem had gotten through safely yesterday. At 8:30 p.m., Dave and I decided to leave for the Knoll with nothing but first aid and some food in an attempt to solve the mystery.

We left camp at a sharp clip, expecting to get stomachaches at every moment after the vast amount of muffins, beef, carrots, beets, potatoes, jam, and macaroni that we'd just finished. We made Bivouac Rock in a rapid one hour and fifty-eight minutes.

The weather was inky black to the south where sombre cloud streamers hung low over Cape Spencer. To the west a vivid red line marked the spot where the sun had set an hour before. A stiff southerly breeze swept soothingly across our trail as we climbed along a veritable staircase of deep, well-kicked footholds already freezing securely. We reached Luncheon Rock at 11:26 p.m., two hours and fifty-six minutes from base camp, beating the all-time record for the climb by hours.

The crust was rotten and breakable and the clouds hung low—mysterious, spooky features draped around the peaks. Snow flurries dimmed Mount Dagelet through the midnight twilight. Mount Crillon rose vaguely before us, gray and almost invisible through drifting mists.

We hurried ahead through fresh tracks, now sure that the men were OK, but wishing to make a certain check on them at the camp. At 11:53 we let out a wild war-whoop and came bearing down on the tents. Bewildered grunts welcomed us, and soon we were inside the cook tent, listening to the faithful purr of the Primus stove as it speedily warmed up the frigid air. All was well. We left at 1:30 and made our uneventful trip back to base camp, arriving at 4:15 a.m. Now off to bed.

TUESDAY, JULY 10

Up at nine o'clock in a wild southeaster: rain, and a hard, cold gale blowing up the lake. We had a lousy breakfast of uncooked cornmeal, yesterday's coffee reheated, and some muffins that were raw and didn't rise—a good radio man is not always a good cook.

Linc and Wok and I had a long council of war about plans for the coming days. We agreed that Linc, Ted, Ad, Hal, and Bem would go to the Knoll tonight, as it had pretty well cleared off by six o'clock. Then we would move all our stuff and our camp from the Knoll and Klooch Corner to the spot in the Great Valley where the highest cache is at present. This will be a very central location for our attempt on Crillon.

Wok and I are to stay here till the plane arrives for our photographic flight over the region, from here up to Yakutat and the St. Elias Range. We also are determined to have our glacier-motion work and surveying well in hand before we leave for the mountain.

Dave and Linc went on a simply ridiculous duck hunt. Two ducks were sighted down the lake after supper, and loud tally-ho's resounded across the cove. They put the canoe in, loaded down with a .22, a .410-gauge shotgun, and a Springfield rifle. The ducks saw them in thirty seconds, and before the hunters had gone more than a hundred yards, the ducks were out of sight over toward the end of the glacier, to the tune of a thousand jeers and boos from camp.

THURSDAY, JULY 12

There was a slight hum in the distance, and in came the plane, piloted by Gene Meyring. We flew off and photographed the whole region. While passing Cape Fairweather at about 3,000 feet, we noticed a remarkable phenomenon. A pit of ice just inland from the cape in the midst of the forest disclosed that the whole cape, except for a narrow, terminal moraine, is completely undermined by ice, with big fir trees growing on top of it.

We noted the position of all the glaciers on the way north. We also made a perfect flight across the Malaspina Glacier, at the foot of 18,000-foot Mount St. Elias. We ran out of gas in our tank halfway across the glacier and glided for twenty to thirty seconds before the other feed line got functioning. These

are always rather nerve-wracking waits, especially in a seaplane over an icefield thirty miles from the nearest water.

As we neared camp on the way home, we flew in close to Crillon, approaching its west face head-on until we almost seemed to hit it. Swinging slightly left, we passed over the staggering northern ridge, and the fantastic Glacier Bay face of the mountain burst upon us. Such wild and terrific cliffs I've never seen before. Smaller than those of St. Elias, Crillon's cliffs are so nearly vertical and so bare and jagged that they present a savage spectacle from the northwest. Dick Goldthwait and I clicked pictures until our fingers were sore. We circled four more times to make a lot of them, under perfect conditions.

Then we glided down toward the Knoll, and we could see that the men had moved the high camp entirely off the Knoll and farther up into the Great Valley. We landed back at our Crillon Lake base camp, six hours after the start of the flight, Dick and I feeling as cold as Greenland.

Now that we have flown around Mount Crillon, we see that it is in excellent shape for climbing, but only for a short time. There is a big crevasse nearly all the way across the approach to the last col (or high pass) near the top. We must strike while the iron is hot.

GREAT VALLEY HIGH CAMP
SATURDAY, JULY 14, 1934

Another perfect day. The reflections of trees and clouds in Crillon Lake as we loaded our packs at 4:20 a.m. were too glorious for words. We were on our way with packs to our high camp in the Great Valley above the Knoll. We made swift progress with about 50-pound loads, and by seven o'clock we'd reached Ptarmigan Dome.

Walking along lightly through the heather and lupine, we approached Bivouac Rock. A ptarmigan and her chicks rushed ahead of us through the heather. We reached the top of the Knoll at 9:10. It was such gorgeous weather that we'd packed nearly stark naked up to that point, and we now put on our clothes for fear of sunburn.

Mount Crillon towers almost 7,000 feet
above as team members approach
our high camp with a big sledge load.

Klooch Corner was a veritable hell of slush and we plodded slowly, warily around it and up into the Great Valley. The route this year is very good—no necessity for roping up and scarcely any crevasses at all. We put on our skis and just after one o'clock, under a roasting sun, we reached camp at the very head of the valley. The thermometer in one of the tents registered 96 degrees.

Our plan is to head for the Crillon Ice Cliff tomorrow at 3:00 a.m. We will sledge up a refuge tent, trail-marking wands, three days of food for six people, gasoline, crampons, etc. We may have lots of trouble with the bergschrund (a big crevasse that separates the glacier from the cliff), and we will be ready for it with a shovel and nine hundred feet of rope.

There was a glorious pink sunset on Crillon. She looks just as aloof as ever, and the summit cone looks very difficult from this side.

SUNDAY, JULY 15

We were up at 3:00 a.m. and off for the South Col (South Pass) with a 450-pound sledge load. The skies were overcast, and snow flurries swept along by a southeast wind filled the air.

We made the base of the col in an hour because there was such a hard crust. We unpacked the load from the sledge and carried everything up the col to 8,100 feet. There is a big crevasse across the col, with only two small snow bridges over it, but they should last ten days or so more. We set up a refuge tent at the very top of the col, where a frigid southeasterly gale was blowing, and filled it with the food and equipment we had carried.

Then we skied down the other side to have a look at the Ice Cliff. It looked almost impossible to scale. There is scarcely any snow at all in the middle of it, only great patches of rotten-looking rocks. At least the crossing of the schrund at the bottom of the cliff will be a snap this year because it is filled in with avalanche debris. Just as we were turning from our inspection, I spied our rope from last year, twisted and broken in the snow. Then it was time to return to high camp in the Great Valley.

MONDAY, JULY 16

We got up at 3:00 a.m. with hopes of a real try at the Ice Cliff, but it was drizzling gently and there was no snow crust at all to walk on. The men who were returning to base camp at Crillon Lake left at about 9:30 in slowly clearing weather. It's a shame that they must leave, but there's lots of work to do down there, and we must have more room for action up here.

We spent the day organizing living and working conditions for six men. Wok and Ted have started to dig a deep grotto in the snow behind camp. They call the grotto the Ratskellar, and it's for storing food and supplies out of the rain, snow, and sun. Hal and I are installed in the cook tent in the utmost comfort. Ad and Bem are across the way.

WEDNESDAY, JULY 18

I crawled outside at 2:00 a.m. and poked my head into a snowstorm. Another try two hours later resulted in the same mournful discovery.

Zowie, but we had a funny breakfast. I ate six bowls of oatmeal and was lying on my bed to recuperate and prepare myself for more labors when Hal asked for some water to wash out his cereal cup. I passed it over and spilled a bit on Wok's foot. He jumped and spilled about half his coffee on his pants and scalded his leg. Whereupon I jumped because I was surprised and spilled even more of Wok's stuff on him. He yelled with pain and leaped high in the air, hitting the tent and knocking down all the water that had condensed on the roof from cooking. Bem came in and we started laughing so hard explaining what happened that Wok kicked over the rest of his coffee. I'm still weak from laughing.

I took a gorgeous ski trip this evening with Hal, Wok, and Bem up to the ridge behind camp. The whole range suddenly came out of the mists. We fought our way up through terrible, breakable crust to the rocks, then took off our skis and sat there in the late evening sun, Crillon soaring before us above three layers of silvery mist, a tiny cloud floating in the lee of its summit. What stupendous cliffs those are that drop off to the South Crillon

The 1934 ascent of Mount Crillon took place from the south. The route followed across the Knoll at 5,600 feet, continued to the final camp at 6,000 feet, then traveled behind the small peak at right before ascending to the summit at 12,728 feet.

Glacier, and what staggering icefalls there are at the head of that valley 3,000 feet below us in the twilight.

We skied back to camp through the most frightful breakable crust imaginable—marvelous practice for jump turns. Now the temperature is about 28 degrees, everything is crusting fast, and the sea of clouds over the ocean seems quite still. The sky above is all clear to the west where a lovely half-moon is rising above Klooch Corner. What a sudden clearoff. Will it be a good day tomorrow?

THURSDAY, JULY 19

Up at 12:20 a.m., out of camp at 2:00. The weather was so perfect and the night so clear and cold and the crust so hard that when we reached the South Col at 3:10 a.m., we decided at once to have a wholehearted stab at the Ice Cliff. We packed up two hundred willow trail-markers, all the rations, one box of still film, nine hundred feet of rope to fix in place on the cliff, three rappel pickets, crampons, and a few other necessities such as a shovel for cornice excavation.

Then we skied to the base of the cliff over the most divine snow imaginable, a hard crust with about two millionths of an inch of soft, fluffy, frost surface. It was a curious sensation to just fly through the almost darkness and not have any idea of the contours of the snow ahead. All we knew was that it was safe to take it straight.

The cliff looked more formidable than ever, studded with outcrops of rock that had never been there at all last year. But although the snow slopes themselves were badly scarred by avalanches, not a single one had recently crossed the schrund, the gap where the glacier meets the mountain itself.

Bem went with me. Ad and Hal followed close behind. Wok and Ted awaited instructions below. Bem carried the rope to fix in place. Hal and Ad each had another rope, plus the shovel and the three pickets. That was all we took, except for three bars of chocolate and some lemon drops. After fixing the rope in place on the Ice Cliff, we expected to be back at the col for lunch.

The schrund was our first surprise. The avalanche trough that had looked so easy several days ago turned out to be a veritable terror of thin blue ice that we couldn't cross at all without a fixed rope from above. A short try convinced me. The left side looked better, so we traversed a bit and cut across a place where avalanches had filled the trough, and then Bem belayed me as I climbed ahead.

The lip of the schrund was almost vertical ice and it meant chipping both foot and handholds. I succeeded at last in stretching my foot around the corner and into the avalanche chute. What a feeling of comfort after that sheer wall of ice. Bem followed after a belay and then we simply rushed up the chute. He let me out a full rope of twenty meters and then I belayed the rope and he pulled himself up it. All went perfectly.

Two-thirds of the way to the rocks, Bem stopped and threw a rope to Ad, belayed it, and brought him and Hal up to us. Then we went ahead, Bem with the rope tied to his belt, till we reached the first rock ledge to the right of the avalanche trough. Then we made it just below a big overhanging rock and the others followed again. We took another rope tied to Bem's belt and continued upward without hesitation, this time up the steep rocks, always to the right of last year's route and parallel to it.

We scarcely had a moment of doubt as to the best route and just roared ahead to the end of the new rope. This we fixed to another ledge two-thirds of the way to the top. Sunrise was on Mount Dagelet, and the sea of clouds over the ocean was flooded with light. The top of Crillon appeared over the ridge to our left. We were at last as high as the lower lip of the plateau above us and going strong.

To our left we spotted one of last year's rappel pickets, standing at a rather cockeyed angle in the snow between two rock ledges. Now we were on a narrow rib, safe from avalanches that could course down the gullies to our right and left.

After fixing this second rope in place, we continued as fast as possible to the top of the buttress, where a fine rock ledge gave us a corking view of the cornice at the very top. Two bits of delicate rock work held us up for only a few minutes. Above us, the edges of the plateau sharply cut the pale blue sky of early morning.

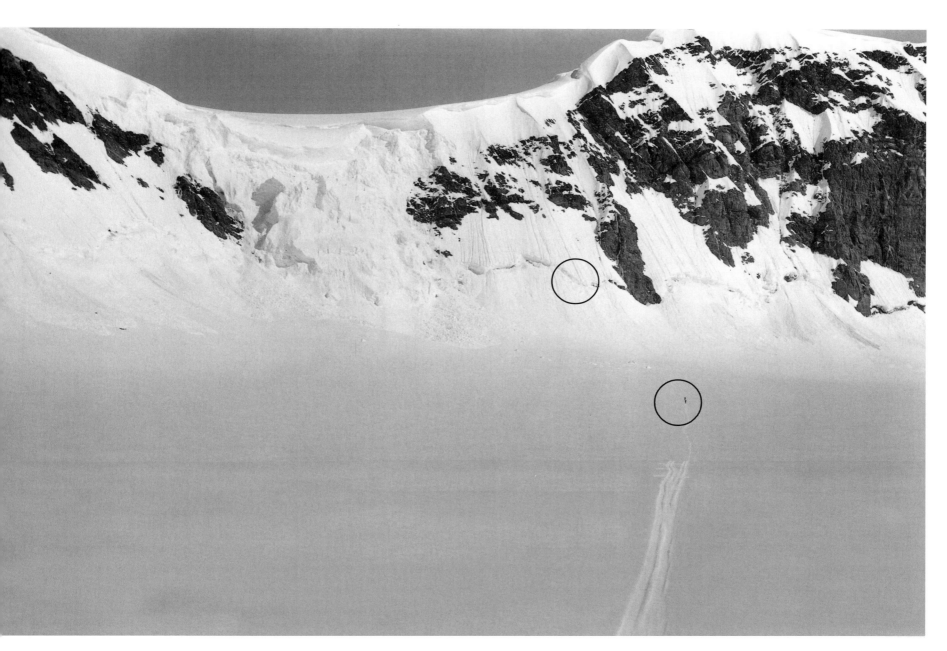

A climber, nearly lost in a vast expanse of white, crosses the snowfield near the Mount Crillon Ice Cliff, while another negotiates the Ice Cliff near its bottom. The 800-foot cliff was a major obstacle to reaching the upper plateau that led leftward toward the summit.

To our left rose Crillon, crystal-like and defiant and sparkling; to our right towered the massive summit of Dagelet, bathed in the full rays of the morning sun. Behind us a sea of clouds stretched endlessly over the ocean to the horizon. Only a short slope remained between us and the cornice. Five minutes of easy climbing through perfect hard snow brought us to a hollow of snow beneath the cornice. After twenty minutes of careful excavating, we were ready to try punching a route through the overhanging snow of the cornice and up onto the plateau.

I clambered on Bem's shoulders, tottering gently as I tried to get an axe-hold in the slope above a tiny gap in the cornice. But I could find no firm spot to jam my ice axe, and I had to descend to my original place beside him and scratch my head for another solution.

I chopped handholds in the vertical snow above us and then drove my axe in above them to steady us as we slowly rose again in our little tumbler's act. This time we were more secure, and I jammed my axe deeply into the hard snow several feet back from the edge of the cornice.

The sun caught me full in the face. The ranges behind Glacier Bay burst into view, and the plateau glittered before me. I jammed the ice axe to the very head, warned Bem to brace himself, and with a last little shove on his shoulder, I clambered out into the mystic country that my fellow climbers and I had left a year ago, expecting never to return. It was inexpressibly marvelous to be there on the great plateau once more, face to face with this grand old peak. Bem followed quickly on my fixed rope after handing up my crampons. We wasted no time. Ad and Hal were hot on our heels.

We had only intended to put the fixed ropes on the Ice Cliff so that we could use them on another day for a full summit attempt. But a council of war changed our plans. The crust on the plateau was solid and smooth. It was only 6:45 in the morning and such a chance to summit Crillon could not be overlooked. Ad and I, as the most experienced climbers, were the logical ones for the attack.

Hal and Bem buckled down to work, excavating a deep trench through the cornice to make the uphill route safer. We yelled down to Wok and Ted and asked them to run back to the South Col for more supplies. They were then to act as a support party and follow us across the plateau with the food and willow wands for marking the route. Not a cloud was in the sky and there was hardly a breath of wind.

The assault now began in earnest. The beautiful day and the presence of a large support party following close on our heels made possible climbing that would otherwise have been out of the question.

Ad and I took all the chocolate and lemon drops and I borrowed Bem's goggles. Then we started for Crillon at top speed. As we rushed across the plateau, all glittering in the brilliant early sun, we planned our route of attack on the summit cone. The great snowfield seemed to melt away beneath us as we dashed ahead. Our only thoughts were about that icy final pyramid that rose above us.

At 8:15 we rested a few moments at 9,600 feet at the foot of the summit slope. Then we started upward again, Ad leading. All went perfectly. The slope was flawless, hard as rock and except for one wide crevasse at about 10,500 feet, quite free of danger. The slope above here steepened rapidly, but by 9:20 we'd reached the upper lip of the great barrier crevasse that we'd recently seen from the airplane.

That plane trip saved us a long detour, for I had the whole route perfectly imprinted on my mind. The grade lessened; crevasses followed each other faster, but always covered with firm snow. The climbing became more difficult because of thick, semi-windpacked snow that we broke through ankle deep. Ad led with a superb pace: slow, steady, short steps, the kind that get one up fast.

The summit cone now rose to our left in a staggering mass of blue ice, white snow, and frost feathers. The route that we'd chosen directly up the ridge looked possible, but we were not yet sure of it. An alternative lay to the left, with a traverse about the summit cone three hundred feet below the top, with the final ascent along the west ridge. We wanted to avoid this if possible. The traverse was very steep and there was obvious danger of starting an avalanche in this loose snow.

The team that attempted Mount Crillon in 1933 successfully climbed the Ice Cliff. Charley Houston (top, right) prepares to climb over the back of Bob Bates in order to reach the base of the cliff, as Ad Carter follows with a load of wooden pickets for jamming into the cliff face as attachment points for ropes.

Mount Crillon's south face rises above a sea of clouds. The climbing route followed the snowfield plateau to the right of the summit.

We made the ridge at 10:25, a good twenty-five minutes ahead of my predicted time from the top of the cliff, which was now way below us—phenomenal time for a walk of four miles and a vertical climb of 3,100 feet. We never rested, but kept relentlessly ahead, always fearing a change in the weather. The powder snow as we neared the top became considerably deeper.

Here and there a bulge of blue ice under the snow warned us that Crillon was in much the same shape as when we tried it a year ago. At eleven o'clock we had traversed under two bulbous gendarmes and were resting in a deep grotto, studded with myriad fantastic frost feathers beneath its sheltered, overhanging southern wall.

It was bitterly cold, with a hard north wind that hummed through the frost feathers and blew little eddies of them down our necks. Clouds were rolling to the north. Mount Fairweather's 15,300-foot peak had disappeared. We knew we must hurry.

We hastily ate a bar of chocolate, munched a few fruit drops, and put on our crampons. Ad's hands were so cold that I had to put his crampons on for him. I had no parka; it was at the bottom of the Ice Cliff. This morning, neither of us had dreamed that we might reach the summit of Crillon today. My ski jacket had always been warm enough, and this time it was to get the acid test. I pulled my light cotton hat tight over my ears and we started off through knee-deep powder, with me now in the lead. Below us on the plateau, in the hot morning sun, we could see four tiny specks approaching the base of the mass of Crillon.

Circling the base of an ice gendarme, we crossed a narrow bridge of snow over a deep crack that acts as a sort of moat or schrund around the summit pyramid. The col between the gendarme and the peak was smooth, hard, and safe. The wind hit us there with a blast. For the first time we could look down on the other side of Crillon. The Johns Hopkins Glacier—a mass of jagged ice pinnacles and fearful bottomless crevasses—wormed its tortuous way below us toward Glacier Bay more than 12,000 feet below.

The summit cone now rose only two hundred feet above us to the left. Its lower end was abrupt and vertical for a dozen feet. A short, delicate traverse above the precipice was necessary before we could start the ridge itself. Powder snow a foot deep covered lower layers of blue ice, and the snow had to be brushed aside before steps could be chopped. This I did leaning over the abyss while Ad belayed me.

Ten minutes' work and we were on the ridge. Here the going was slow but steady. Every time I brushed the loose, new snow off the icy ridge, cold snow blew up into my face, swirled down my neck, and speckled my goggles. We progressed by inches. I slowly cut steps, first balanced on one foot, then on the other, that incredible cliff down to our right.

The other climbers had disappeared from view behind a ledge below us. Then the mist closed in. All we could see was swirling snow and a narrow, knife-edged ridge rising before us and melting out of sight into the fog.

At 12:20 the grade seemed to lessen. A spectral ridge of white appeared from the clouds to our right. Our steps could now be further apart. My left leg no longer swung in free air between footholds, nor did I lean precariously any more against the icy ridge. I planted my axe securely for the last time, and Ad came to my side from the narrow ridge below.

I pointed ahead and Ad grinned: "Oh, if Bob Bates and Walt Everett and Harold Paumgarten could only be with us now." We both felt that way about our partners from the year before. Then, too exhausted to make a dash for it, we slowly plodded a hundred feet up a gently rolling surface of deep, feathery snow. At ten seconds before 12:30, we planted our axes atop the peak of Mount Crillon and shook hands until our wrists ached.

With the weather deteriorating, our stay on top was short. We took a couple of jubilant pictures with Ad's little camera since mine was somewhere on the slope at least a thousand feet below. Then we started the descent after only ten minutes of the best exultation that two men could have ever had.

The ridge was worse descending than climbing. We took care such as I've never taken in my life as we backed off from the spacious summit. The steps had already filled again with powder snow, and while I belayed Ad, he kicked

The final route segment to the summit cone of Mount Crillon followed this snowfield, close to the right-hand cliffs that drop 7,000 feet to the Johns Hopkins Glacier. The last 200 vertical feet went up the narrow, knife-edged ridge directly at the top of the cliff.

each step free of snow. Then I followed while he belayed. At one o'clock we were once more in our little snow grotto, and at one-thirty we'd reached easy, safe going once more.

Crillon was conquered and we could say so safely now. The ridge was behind us and the only obstacles that lay ahead were the miles of weary plateau travel followed by the delicate descent of the Ice Cliff.

We met the others above the barrier crevasse at about 11,000 feet. The weather clearly made it unwise for them to go on to the top. Plunging downward, we came out of the mist just below 11,000 feet. There we all sat down in the deep, sticky snow and ate a huge meal. The ocean lay below us and all the rest of the range was clear as crystal. A local windstorm enveloped only the tip-top of Crillon.

The descent of the Ice Cliff was hell, as expected. Bem, Wok, and Ad went down first on one rope, followed by Ted, Hal, and me on another. Our rope team simply crept downward, being afraid of hitting the men below us with loose stones. Slush avalanches coursed by all around us. A huge block of ice fell off the slope to our right, and the concussion shook the mountain.

That cliff is nerve-wracking at best, and we all heaved a great sigh of relief as we slipped down across the schrund on the fixed rope and finally reached our skis. No more dangers lay between us and camp except the South Col crevasses. And those were nothing after what we'd already been through.

We pulled into the refuge tent at the South Col at 8:30 p.m. and piled up our boots, the camera, and the ropes and crampons there. Then we had a most glorious ski descent back to our 6,000-foot camp. After ten perfectly grand minutes flying like the wind, we came to a stop in front of camp at nine o'clock, the end of a marvelous day. We took nineteen hours and forty minutes to reach the top and return. We were too tired to eat much meat, but we just guzzled vegetables and, of course, the special can of caviar that we'd brought along for this thrilling moment.

We'd reached the top of Mount Crillon!

FRIDAY, JULY 20

We spent the morning fooling around camp, mainly working on the camera— and to my horror I discovered that the lens on the still camera has been loose all this summer so far. All the cliff pictures yesterday must be ruined, and all those that we took on the lower parts of Crillon. What a dreadful discovery. I've mended it now, but I have little faith that the pictures we took today were in good focus. All that we have in hand to prove we reached the top of Crillon are the ones taken with Ad's vest-pocket Kodak, made on a fogbound snowdrift.

The only solution is to climb Crillon again, and to do it immediately, while yesterday's tracks are still there, and pray that the weather will hold for just one more day. And this time we'll bring not only Ad's trusty little Kodak, but my repaired large camera and our big 35mm movie camera.

SATURDAY, JULY 21

After almost no sleep and a miserable little breakfast, Wok, Ad, and I left camp again at 12:35 a.m., determined to climb Crillon a second time, with 35 pounds of cameras and film. I felt really discouraged, climbing all the way to the ridge behind camp, breaking through half-frozen crust to my knees on every other step. However, when we reached the South Col, we discovered that we were making record time.

Skiing downward, we reached the base of the Ice Cliff in a twinkling. My, what time we made up that almost thousand feet of fixed ropes. We climbed together except in a few delicate places, and we moved so quickly that, when we reached the cornice, we found we'd gone much faster than Ad and I had done two days before.

The once-slushy plateau was frozen like rock. Roped together, we hiked jauntily along abreast for an hour and a half, arriving at the beginning of the steeper part of the ascent at 5:15. The sunrise over the ocean, now far below us, was more beautiful than ever before.

Wok led up the ever-steeper slope. The frozen steps of two days before were a boon. We were so scared that this gorgeous weather would change, we scarcely dared stop for even a moment to take a still picture, but here and there we took a short movie. At 9:15 we reached 12,300 feet at the base of the first steep rise toward the summit and had a quick bit of lunch. It was so hot in the shadowless sunlight that it was a tremendous effort to climb. There wasn't even the slightest breeze, and we sat, sweltering, with our shirts off.

We ate and rested for twenty minutes, then left all of our extra clothes, taking with us only some toffee and a bar of chocolate. We wore only sleeveless shirts, and carried parkas to wear only if they were needed. Wok led to the grotto. There we put on our crampons again, and I took the lead once more as we tackled the final ridge.

Now there was a little breeze, and our old steps were lost in new hard-packed and crusted snow. The lack of wind made the going infinitely easier and safer than before, but the final icy crest of the last fifty feet was just as delicate and dramatic. At last, at exactly 10:45 a.m., the grade lessened and we triumphantly climbed out onto the top.

It was cool—not at all cold—with a little breeze swirling bits of loose snow into our faces. We put on our parkas, but I can always say I climbed the final ridge of Crillon in a sleeveless jersey.

Mount Fairweather, St. Elias, Logan, and even far-off Lucania stood out clear and sharp to the north. Not even a tiny cloud in sight anywhere. To the east lay Glacier Bay, its waters so calm that all of the peaks around it were reflected in every detail in its iceberg-dotted, mirror-like waters. To the south, Icy Strait lay motionless, like a mill pond. The great plateau and nearby Mount La Perouse shimmered in the midday heat. And there was Cenotaph Island, sitting in the still waters of Lituya Bay. How many times we've strolled the rocky shores of that island, looking longingly 12,000 feet above us to the lofty spot where Ad and Wok and I stood today.

The first thing we did was to have a terrific handshake and eat a small package of toffee given to us by Bob Bates. He and Charley Houston had stood ever-so-near to this spot only a year before. Then we unrolled an American flag and a Harvard banner and lashed them to a ski pole that Ad had carried to the top for this purpose. Then we took pictures till our fingers ached from changing film.

This photographic orgy completed, I did something I hadn't dared to do in the fog of two days earlier. I crawled over to the northwest edge of the summit, well belayed by both Ad and Wok, punctured a hole in the cornice, and looked down more than 5,000 feet, virtually straight down to the head of Crillon Glacier.

We spent over an hour on top, then headed back down, much happier than anybody else, anywhere in Alaska, at that moment. It seemed as if we got back to the top of the Ice Cliff in no time, but it was a miserable descent, wallowing almost knee-deep in slush all the way. I led till I couldn't move another inch, then Ad took over, then Wok. The glare of the sun was oppressive, and even in our shirtsleeves the heat was dreadful. Luckily a sweet little northerly breeze followed us all the way.

We didn't hesitate at the crest of the Ice Cliff, but headed right over its edge without a moment's break. The worst climbing accidents occur on the descent, right after a thrilling climb. So we kept the rope tight between us and reached the bottom in less than an hour.

Our pals had spied us coming. Bem met us on skis, carrying canteens full of cool water. We got back to camp at 5:00 p.m. What a marvelous feeling. We'd climbed Crillon twice in three days. And this time we'd done it in just about seventeen hours—much faster than the first time.

SUNDAY, JULY 22

Bem and I slept in the cook tent last night and couldn't resist the temptation to get up early and have a good, big breakfast. We decided to leave immediately for base camp, as the airplane is expected soon and we want to send out more mail, plus lots of summit film.

Yesterday's afternoon slush had crusted over so much that Bem and I were able to ski down to the Knoll in barely an hour. But the sky was ominous with

Mount Crillon's northwest face plunges 8,500 feet to the North Crillon Glacier. From the summit, the climbers could peer down this staggering precipice of rock and ice.

high lenticular wind clouds to the east. The upper Knoll Ridge was miserable, as we were descending for the last time and had to carry both our skis and ski boots. But the lupine was more beautiful than ever; we trod through it knee-deep as we crossed Ptarmigan Dome. Another wonderful ski descent and we were back in the land of green trees, twittering birds, and bubbling brooks. Everything down here seems so soft and quiet and friendly.

CRILLON LAKE BASE CAMP
MONDAY, JULY 23, 1934

Up at 5:30. Perfect weather again, despite last night's evil omens. Not a cloud in the sky, and the barometer continues its steady rise. The heat has been frightful—above 80 degrees almost all day. At 4:30 we went over to the spring and dug a bathtub.

The dispatch radioed by Dave Putnam to the *New York Times* after our first ascent produced a big headline: "Crillon Is Scaled by College Party."

The byline read, "By Bradford Washburn, Leader of the Harvard-Dartmouth Mount Crillon Expedition."

My article told the world that "Adams Carter and the writer, forming the advance climbing party . . . reached the summit of Mount Crillon, the highest hitherto unscaled peak of the Fairweather Range in Alaska."

Radiograms arrived, including these from my family:

"Thrilled and delighted over glorious news Crillon conquest. Love. Father and Mother."

"Cheers. Congratulations. We are all one broad smile. Heaps of love. Sis."

TUESDAY, JULY 24

Linc and Russ left for the Knoll to bring down the big camera and tripod. Dick took pictures of Bem and me skiing. Russ killed three ptarmigan on Ptarmigan Dome, and we've just had them for supper. Bed at 10:30. Gorgeous moon. Wire from Juneau says airplane will pick up Dick Goldthwait sometime tomorrow.

WEDNESDAY, JULY 25

Dick and I retrieved his ice-depth recording instruments from well up at the corner of South Crillon Glacier. His work up there has been a great success. The ice is 840 feet deep! We had to hurry all the way so as not to miss the plane. We noticed that the glacier had advanced a lot in the last two years. It's invading the forest all along this edge.

Then we had a good swim in the lake, cavorting all around the icebergs. Made some fudge. Wrote long letter to the family. Waited in vain for the airplane. Also got a telegram from home, jubilant about our second ascent of Crillon.

THURSDAY, JULY 26

At last Gene Meyring and the plane arrived, and I took off with him on a last photographic flight. Much, much better weather than during our previous flight. Low fog drifted along the coast as we slowly climbed over Lituya Bay and Bald Mountain to get pictures of areas not yet accurately mapped. Then we climbed steadily, passing La Perouse Glacier and so near to the top of the Knoll that we were able to drop a note to our men picking up the last of our stuff there. The film tin that held the message was well weighted with fudge!

We then made three circles around the top of Crillon, getting closer each time. We flew through a cloudless sky, in the smoothest air imaginable. On the third swing, we got so close that we could see our footsteps, and our flags on the summit stood out clearly.

FRIDAY, AUGUST 10

The last dozen days of the expedition were spent in long, low-altitude hikes which covered every detail of the terrain between Lituya Bay and Crillon Lake, not only to make certain that our new map of the area would be very accurate, but also to complete our knowledge of its geology.

After all, aside from making a new map, the important ice-depth studies by Dick Goldthwait and our research on the movement of South Crillon Glacier proved that our research program was of much greater importance than the first ascent of the area's highest peak.

It was time to leave Crillon Lake, and this last day turned out to be explosive. Gene Meyring and his beautiful Lockheed Vega airplane arrived at base camp in the afternoon. We had been told that the unused dynamite from Dick's ice-depth work should not be just left there. Gene was not too eager to fly this stuff back to Juneau. So we devised an unusual and rather thrilling way to get rid of it.

When we established this camp, we had made a big toilet at a site between two large spruce trees. Russ had brought along a beautiful new toilet seat, which we installed on two long poles, fixed halfway between the trees. Directly below the seat we dug a deep hole. During the summer, it became almost filled with you-know-what.

We had 125 sticks of unused dynamite. As we were about to abandon camp for good, we agreed we should place all of this dynamite on top of the gigantic pyramid of you-know-what in the bottom of that hole.

While we put an electrical connection in one of the sticks of dynamite and strung out a long wire to a cutbank beside the lake, Meyring's crew chief moved the airplane to a safe place 200 yards southward on the lakeshore. Then all of us cowered in a nearby safe spot and pushed the lever.

This was not an explosion. It was a gigantic roar!

The two trees which held the seat were laid flat on the ground, all of their branches stripped clean. A huge sheet of flame rose high above the lake. Russ insisted he clearly saw his toilet seat, swirling around, at least a thousand feet in the sky.

This display of fireworks brought the 1934 Harvard-Dartmouth Mount Crillon Expedition to a never-to-be-forgotten end.

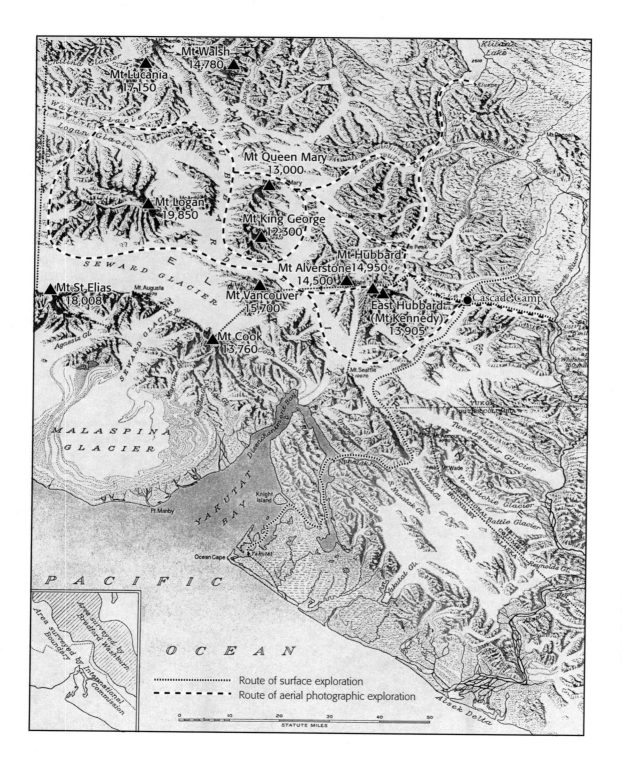

The National Geographic Society Yukon Expedition of 1935 explored—by foot or by air reconnaissance and photography—an unmapped area of more than 6,000 square miles of Canada's Yukon Territory and southeastern Alaska. *Map surveyed by Bradford Washburn and International Boundary Commission. Edited by Bradford Washburn and Dr. Erwin Raisz. Reproduction courtesy of National Geographic Society.*

EXPEDITION DIARY II

NATIONAL GEOGRAPHIC SOCIETY YUKON EXPEDITION *1935*

To Andrew M. Taylor, a tower of strength and competence
throughout the exploration of this frigid wilderness.

BRADFORD WASHBURN'S NATIONAL GEOGRAPHIC SOCIETY Yukon Expedition came about almost by accident.

During the summer of 1934, Washburn and Bob Bates began to develop plans for a first ascent of remote and lofty Mount Lucania, a 17,150-foot peak in Canada's Yukon Territory. After word began to leak out about their goal, Washburn received a call from Bill Ladd of the American Alpine Club in New York. Ladd told Washburn that the distinguished mountaineer Walter Wood was already deep in plans for an ascent of Lucania—and that it would be appropriate to let him make the first attempt on this great peak.

With no little regret, the "youngsters" acquiesced. The Lucania Expedition, sponsored by the National Geographic Society, now became the Yukon Expedition. At that time, the area south of Lucania was a vast blank on the map: 6,000 square miles of glaciated wilderness on the border of Canada and Alaska. The new objective was to explore and map as much as possible of this wild desert of rock and ice.

The 1935 expedition was pure exploration, with no summit as the goal. Even before Washburn and his team set out on foot, discoveries were made from the air. Washburn telegraphed his findings to the National Geographic Society, and the information was swiftly publicized in the *New York Times*. The newspaper reported that Washburn had discovered a new glacier, fifty miles in length, descending from the peak of Mount Hubbard into the Alsek Valley of the Yukon; found two large peaks between Mount Hubbard and Mount Lucania; and learned that the Hubbard Glacier, thought to be thirty miles in length, was at least twice that long.

Once the aerial photos were taken and developed, the mapping expedition began in earnest, working from a base camp on newly discovered Lowell Glacier. Despite seemingly endless blizzards, the expedition surveyed a large region and also explored the flanks of Mount Alverstone, Mount Hubbard, and East Hubbard (later named Mount Kennedy, in honor of the assassinated U.S. president).

As it turned out, the reluctant decision to change objectives from the Mount Lucania climb to Yukon exploration was a blessing in disguise. Walter Wood failed in his attempt to climb Lucania. However, aerial reconnaissance by the Yukon expedition yielded a detailed knowledge of the route to the summit. On July 9, 1937, Washburn and Bates made the first ascent of Mount Lucania.

Photos by Bradford Washburn for the National Geographic Society

Courtesy of the National Geographic Society

Members of the Yukon Expedition team and their pilot pose at Carcross, Yukon Territory, at the start of their adventure. They are (back row, from left) Andy Taylor, Brad Washburn, pilot Everett Wasson, and Ome Daiber, and (front row) Ad Carter, Harty Beardsley, and Bob Bates. Missing from the photo is Jack Haydon, later to join the party with a dog-team.

NATIONAL GEOGRAPHIC SOCIETY YUKON EXPEDITION, 1935

Bradford (Brad) Washburn (leader), of Cambridge, Massachusetts

Robert H. (Bob) Bates, of Philadelphia, Pennsylvania

Hartness (Harty) Beardsley, of Springfield, Vermont

Adams (Ad) Carter, of Newtonville, Massachusetts

Ome Daiber, of Seattle, Washington

Jack Haydon, of Kluane Lake, Yukon, Canada

Andrew M. (Andy) Taylor, of Tompkins Corner, New York

CARCROSS, YUKON, CANADA
TUESDAY, FEBRUARY 26, 1935

A perfect day—not a cloud from sunrise to sunset. We took off with pilot Everett Wasson in the Fairchild FC-2W2 at 7:50, bound to explore the St. Elias Range.

I have never seen such a glorious morning. The sun had just risen when we started down the runway marked by spruce boughs stuck in the snow on Lake Bennett. Smoke circled lazily from the houses of Carcross—once called Caribou Crossing.

By 8:15 we could see Mount Crillon and Mount Fairweather clearly as we flew along at 12,000 feet. Mount Hubbard rose far ahead of us, with Mount Logan hidden behind. The shadows were deep and beautiful and occasional soft mists hung in the valleys. Neither Andy Taylor nor I have ever seen such rough country in our lives and we've seen plenty of roughness! A forced landing would simply be curtains, but our old Wasp engine purred beautifully on without a falter.

We crossed Mush Lake, Bates Lake (not named after our Bob Bates), and the Alsek River, and Crillon and Fairweather began to merge and settle lower on the horizon to the south. An immense glacier appeared ahead, finding its source right beside Mount Alverstone and Mount Hubbard and going all the way to the Alsek River, now at our feet. No mortal man has ever seen this before—one of the greatest glaciers in North America. The late winter is the perfect time of year to explore a place like this, when the deep winter snow

has covered most of the crevasses. Travel on the ground is safer and airplane landings easier.

We passed over Hubbard Col (Pass) at the head of this glacier. The col stood at about 10,000 feet in elevation. At its end a colossal cliff dropped from Hubbard and Alverstone to the Hubbard Glacier—which in turn goes all the way through to Mount Logan in a ten-mile-wide valley. Mount Vancouver was stunning and terrific, utterly impossible from this side—

huge shadowy walls of cascading ice for 10,000 feet above the smooth, low valley of the Hubbard Glacier.

We swung back down our great new glacier (which we later named the Lowell Glacier, after President A. Lawrence Lowell of Harvard College) and found a possible landing place for later. Then we turned north, crossing three more huge glaciers that dump into the Alsek River and finally came out down the Kaskawulsh Glacier to the tiny village of Kluane, nestled among the hills, still shadowy despite its being after noon. We met in Kluane with Andy's old friend Jack Haydon to discuss the need for dogs for our expedition.

On the way back to Carcross, after more flying over the Hubbard Glacier, we finally descended the Lowell Glacier valley to the Alsek River, crossed Bates Lake, and pulled into Carcross at 4:45 with only about five gallons of gas left. I shall never forget seeing the ocean glittering beyond the settlement of Yakutat. It was a real thrill to see that dear old sea again after such bewildering masses of snow and ice for nearly seven hours. This was one of the greatest exploratory flights of recent years in this continent: We saw thousands of square miles of country never before seen by anyone.

Our plan now is to send in a load of supplies and gear with Andy and Everett and to land it as far up the Lowell Glacier as possible. The area of Mount

Hubbard is our logical goal—it looks possible to make the 10,000-foot col north of it with two dog teams in three weeks or so. We'll survey the Lowell Glacier and the Alsek River valley to Bates Lake, I guess. Andy will go over to Kluane and order the dogs from Haydon tomorrow. He also believes that he can get us Haydon's son, also named Jack, to go with us as dog-team driver, plus a good freight sled.

WEDNESDAY, FEBRUARY 27

Fourteen degrees below zero. It was storming on Mount Hubbard all day, and now it's clouding over fast here in Carcross. I guess we've had our luck on our first reconnaissance flight, and we'll have to wait a bit for more beautiful weather. Ome Daiber and I developed some of yesterday's pictures after lunch. Ome is an experienced mountaineer from Seattle, and owner of that city's best ski and climbing equipment store. Jack Haydon, now to be our dog driver, will be ready to fly to our base camp anytime we fly over to get him at Kluane. He's going to charge us $5 per day for his services, including six dogs and a big sled.

Bob Bates, Ad Carter, and Harty Beardsley arrived on the afternoon train. Bob and Ad, both Harvard friends of mine, had been together on our 1933 expedition to Mount Crillon in Southeast Alaska. And Ad and I reached the summit of Crillon together in 1934. Harty was a recent graduate of Dartmouth College and a competent outdoorsman.

We've been eating practically nothing but moose in one form or another, either steaks or roast or liver for every meal. The Caribou Hotel manager killed a big moose in the fall and he plans to serve it as the only hotel food till spring.

THURSDAY, FEBRUARY 28

The boys have been busy all day straightening out the stuff in the warehouse. Andy Taylor has been chopping tent poles and I have written an article and telegraphed it to the National Geographic Society in Washington, D.C. The weather is thickening up more tonight and it looks as if we will be held up here for several more days. But it's great to have the fellows all together again. They are a grand crew.

Andy is superb and will be a great helper, even though he's sixty years old. He was a member of the party that made the first ascent of Mount Logan (19,430 feet high) in 1925. At twenty-four, I'm the second oldest member of this party. They're all singing downstairs now and I must join them for a big sing-song. There is nothing like the spirit of the north to knit real friendships.

SUNDAY, MARCH 3

Stormy and windy all day. We had supper at the Simmons house. He greeted Bob and me as we entered, covered with blizzard snow: "You boys look as if you need a hot-buttered-rum enema!" We had a long bull session, then we had a big poll to see how many flush toilets there are in the Yukon. Aubrey Simmons claimed there are no more than a dozen and named them all.

MONDAY, MARCH 4

Every box is packed and ready to go. All we want now is good weather. We plan to fly in Andy, Ome, Ad, and Harty and leave them on our big, new Lowell Glacier tomorrow if the weather permits.

TUESDAY, MARCH 5

A perfect day all day, but oh, how cold. We got up at six o'clock for a 7:00 a.m. start for the glacier, but it was 26 degrees below zero and it took till 8:50 to get the big Fokker Super Universal plane started. We made the Lowell Glacier in an hour and twenty minutes on a glorious morning. Mount Hubbard and Mount Alverstone were tipped with long, feathery plumes of wind-driven powder snow.

At our campsite, the thermometer stood at 45 degrees below zero, and believe me, we had to scurry to get the plane unloaded before the engine froze up. Everett Wasson, the pilot, left at 10:30 amid a whirl of flying snow and was soon lost behind the Alsek River and the faraway hills east of it.

A frigid breeze blew down the glacier and hurried us in our work. A Logan tent went up in a jiffy, and then the big base-camp wall tent that

Courtesy of the National Geographic Society

Brad Washburn gets some exercise on a day off at Carcross.

looks as if we'd used it at every camp for a year. Two more Logan tents went up after a frugal lunch of nuts, cake, and hot coffee from a heaven-sent thermos bottle.

Everett arrived with the second planeload of supplies from Carcross at 3:20. He and I were then off almost immediately for the flight back to Carcross.

WEDNESDAY, MARCH 6

Unsettled weather today. It's twenty below zero at 10:00 p.m. bedtime. Our big Fairchild K-3B camera won't work and we plan to use the smaller Fairchild F-8, which takes twenty-five 5-by-7-inch photos in each roll. It's much less bulky to handle.

THURSDAY, MARCH 7

It was a cold, cloudless morning at 15 degrees below, and the flight to our camp on the Lowell Glacier was fully as inspiring as ever. We now have a new and very competent pilot, Bob Randall. Every time we cross the mountains we see new and more interesting and beautiful things. The millions of old cirques and jagged, crenelated ridges and sharp peaks will always have new secrets no matter how many times we cross over them.

We landed at the camp with a huge load at 9:10 a.m., unloaded in a jiffy, and were off again at 9:30. We flew in circles over camp until we reached 10,000 feet and then started southward and westward around Mount Hubbard. Two enormous glaciers course southward from Mount Hubbard toward the Alsek River between Lowell Glacier and Nunatak Fiord, making the total of glaciers that we've discovered to be five south of Kluane alone.

It looks very much as if we'll be able to sledge through to Yakutat at the end of our expedition, coming out down the Art Lewis and Nunatak Glaciers. That would be some stunt if we could pull it off.

After circling several times for pictures of those new glaciers, we swung northward up the Hubbard Glacier. We took a look behind Mount Vancouver to take some pictures of its stupendous west face—also some of 13,800-foot Mount Cook.

Courtesy of the National Geographic Society

Brad Washburn stands before the Fairchild FC-2W2 ski plane used by the National Geographic Society Yukon Expedition. Aerial reconnaissance and photography from this plane opened up a world of unexplored glaciers and mountains.

As we crossed the immense expanse of the Seward Glacier, we got magnificent pictures of Mount St. Elias and Mount Logan. I have never seen such utterly colossal cliffs as that south wall of Logan and the northerly crags of St. Elias. And anyone who thinks that the Duke of Abruzzi had it easy in 1897 during the first ascent of 18,000-foot St. Elias can just go and have a try for himself.

Nobody else in the world has ever seen such sights as we packed into those four fleeting hours. The valley of the Chitina River loomed grey, cold, and desolate below us to the left. When we were on the back side of Mount Logan, Bob Randall asked me: "Where the hell are we?" Apparently I was the only one in that airplane who knew the way home.

We might just as well have gone into a nose dive and committed suicide if the motor had failed. The chance of ever getting found in there, even after making a perfect landing, was zero. We had no radio, and nobody had the slightest idea of where we were going since we were exploring an unmapped wilderness. We'd have just sat in the plane, eaten our emergency rations, and then frozen to death. We were more than a hundred miles in every direction from the nearest semblance of humanity.

We headed for base camp on the Lowell Glacier. We made a perfect landing and straggled into the big tent to get some coffee. Andy and Bob Randall flew off for Kluane and returned with Jack Haydon and six dogs in one yelping mass in the back of the Fairchild. They had had a terrible time getting the dogs into the plane, but it was a cinch to get them out. We clapped ten gallons of gas into the airplane and flew back to Carcross.

FRIDAY, MARCH 8

The clouds of last night vanished, so we sent Bob Randall off alone with a 900-pound load, with instructions to land that stuff at the left side of the icefall, about ten miles above our present base camp. Bob returned after a very successful flight. He set the load down exactly where we showed him on my new pictures and then took Ad and another load up there so that he'd also know just where the stuff was left.

It's a perfect location for our new base camp, just at the fork of the glaciers

Courtesy of the National Geographic Society

The temperature, with a raw breeze, was minus 30 degrees Fahrenheit when this ski plane landed with more supplies for the lower camp on Lowell Glacier.

at an altitude of 5,000-odd feet and nicely sheltered below the southern edge of the icefall. That is exactly where Everett Wasson should have landed us at first. He was just plain scared of glaciers. Bob Randall isn't. Bob has given us a real base camp—even if we still have to sledge at least twenty more miles to get really close to Mount Hubbard. We trust that he will do all of our flying from now on.

The clouds are rolling in fast now, and it looks like another storm. But that's OK. We can use a couple of days here in Carcross to straighten out the last details.

WEDNESDAY, MARCH 13

It looks as if we'll never get out of here again. Now the weather is good, cloudless all day, but no planes are available for a day or two.

MONDAY, MARCH 18

Terrific storm all day with the temperature hovering around 20 above. Snow and wind so thick and hard you could scarcely see a hundred feet at times. It must be an inferno out on the glacier where the others are camped.

FRIDAY, MARCH 22

At sunset last night it cleared off completely in a most miraculous way. It was 8 below zero when I rose at 4:15 a.m. A thick, frosty mist hung over the lake. Bob Randall flew down and we finally got the frost mostly off the wings, and the stinking old fish (food for the dogs) packed away.

When we flew over the original lower camp, all we could see was one lonely Logan tent—nobody in sight. They must have all packed up to the new campsite. We saw their trail here and there on the way up the glacier.

We finally came down in beautiful sunlight near our new base camp, which soon came to be known as Cascade Camp. We taxied toward the icefall for some distance and then Andy and the dogs met us. Thank heaven camp has been established up here. I explained to Andy how to put up our new 6-by-6-by-6-foot prefabricated hut that we flew out on this load.

When we took off again, Bob had to circle through very bumpy air for twenty minutes before we could strike out homeward at 12,000 feet, above the clouds. The air was terribly rough all the way back to Carcross. God only knows when we'll be able to fly back to Cascade Camp. Soon we'll have more snow—the barometer is going down, down, down. If we can't get camp completed pretty soon, we'll have a terrible time getting our surveying work done before the spring thaw begins.

CASCADE CAMP ON LOWELL GLACIER
THURSDAY, MARCH 28, 1935

We're all together at last in a dandy camp, safe, and it's not very windy. A glorious day. This morning, Bob Randall and I flew out of Carcross at eleven o'clock, cheering loudly and zooming the town.

Our little hut is up, and we'll finish it tomorrow. Weather now is clear. Zeus, but it's grand to be here. There's great good humor and swell morale considering the damned mess of delays we've been through.

FRIDAY, MARCH 29

Andy, Bob Bates, and I worked on our hut made of insulating board all morning. Ome and Ad took loads up over the icefall and placed a survey flag on the rocky ledge behind camp.

Ad and I did our first paperwork in our new little shack. It's a perfect place to work—so warm inside that one can write easily, even though it's 4-below outside. This hut will make all the difference in the world while we're preparing the results of our survey work.

SATURDAY, MARCH 30

Slept marvelously in the little hut. Ome and Bob and Ad spent the whole day till midafternoon on skis investigating the beginning of our route south of Mount Hubbard heading toward the settlement of Yakutat on the coast.

Andy and I broke the trail six miles or so gently upward along the great valley of upper Lowell Glacier through rather loose snow. That valley is a stunner—great towering peaks and glimpses of Hubbard and Alverstone on the left and huge peaks ahead. But it's a long one. You can walk for hours and never seem to get anywhere at all. We crossed the tracks of a fox and a goat, bound across the glacier from and to God knows where or why.

A grand supper. Golly, codfish cakes are good—and currant jelly. After supper Andy and I carefully cleaned our surveying instrument, the theodolite, preparing it for a big season of work. Theodolites have been used for many, many years to measure vertical and horizontal angles accurately, and ours, loaned to us by Harvard's Institute for Geographical Exploration, is an excellent British Tavistock instrument.

It's 15 degrees outside, and gentle northern lights are silhouetting the icefall in the sky.

SUNDAY, MARCH 31

In the hut, Bob Bates and I slept like logs and were awakened by the chirping of a flock of snowbirds flitting around outside the window. The sun streaming in made it seem almost like spring.

Ome and Andy went up the valley, putting in willow wands to mark the trail. I found our little radio in a box and set it up. Now I'm listening to church music in Cincinnati, Ohio! It's a good receiver. I only wish that we had a transmitter. Nobody but Bob Randall has the slightest idea of where we are. Harty and Jack pulled in this evening at six after sledging two loads all the way up from the original lower camp.

MONDAY, APRIL 1

The dogs took the day off. Bob Bates and Andy made a trip across the valley and put a survey target on the station across on the other side of the icefall. Ome and I measured our baseline, the starting point of our survey— a great triumph as we came out perfect in two tapings, only six-tenths of an inch off.

Those endless delays in Carcross haven't helped us at all. Now we have to try to do three months' work in two, but we'll do it somehow.

Courtesy of the National Geographic Society

Expedition headquarters at Cascade Camp was set up next to the Lowell Glacier Icefall at an elevation of about 5,000 feet.

55

TUESDAY, APRIL 2

Ome and I surveyed all afternoon from the Cascade Station on the bedrock ledge above camp. After establishing one more station, the map will really begin to take form. We had a terrible time working in the middle of the day as the theodolite tripod sinks into the snow from the sun's heat.

Star sights will be the only way to get our exact position here. For that, we need to know the precise time. We got swell time signals on the radio— yesterday, this morning, and this evening. We certainly should be able to fix our position nicely.

THURSDAY, APRIL 4

Clear and cool all day. Not over 30 and not below 20. Perfect. After lunch, Harty, Ome, and I skied over to the other side of our icefall to survey—a nine-mile round-trip. It was a magnificent view from this new survey station, overlooking all of the three great valleys and in full view of Hubbard and Alverstone. It was icy there, but we finished our job and left at five, reaching camp at seven.

Ad and Jack just returned from sledging a load eight or nine miles up the glacier to a high new cache.

Another magnificent supper. We're living like kings.

FRIDAY, APRIL 5

Bob and Ad put in a survey station near Triangle Peak, a sixteen-mile walk. I stayed in camp all day, figuring the map out. The map is progressing very well. Lots more work to do, though. To bed at 10:30 after a big Ovaltine orgy.

SATURDAY, APRIL 6

Jack and I took the six dogs and reconnoitred down the whole valley over the last height of land to where we could see a wonderful gateway leading out to Yakutat.

The vast expanse of the Hubbard Glacier disappeared to the right, and to the left a narrow valley plunged beneath a sea of sombre clouds, bound for the icy waters of Nunatak Fiord—the route we'll probably take us out to tidewater at the end of the expedition. The snow was hard as rock, a marvelous dog trail.

We repositioned our last survey station on a little snow dome that we call The Mound, about seven hundred feet above the valley. This put us at an overall altitude of about 6,300 feet. The job completed, we left almost at once to return to camp. The home journey was lovely in the changing evening light, feathery streamers of mist draping Hubbard at the back of its great valley. Will this glorious weather hold?

SUNDAY, APRIL 7

The sky is now fast clouding up and it looks like a storm before long. The roof of our subterranean storage grotto, dug in a huge snowdrift behind camp, has practically collapsed. Andy and Ome have put in more than a day's worth of work in building a new and luxurious one. Dug deep into the hillside, it looks like the tomb of Rameses II. All it lacks is a Sphinx at each side of the door.

MONDAY, APRIL 8

It snowed lightly at camp all afternoon. We had a frozen bottle of India ink, and when we tried to thaw it out on top of the kerosene stove, it exploded and simply bathed the whole hut and all of Harty, me, and the map. In fact, alas, it ruined the whole left side of my lovely new caribou jacket that was made for me by a native lady in Carcross.

I am regularly reminded what a godsend this hut is. It's warm and cozy and bright in here and one would never think that we were twenty miles from dry land up a glacier in the Yukon Territory.

TUESDAY, APRIL 9

Blizzard all day with the temperature at about 25 degrees. Almost a foot of snow has fallen since last night. The dogs certainly lead a comfortable life. They simply curl up and sleep right in the snow and get completely buried without minding it a bit. There's nothing left to do in weather like this but write letters and read the good old *Reader's Digest*.

THURSDAY, APRIL 11

What a storm—a veritable inferno of blowing, cutting snow such as I've never seen. We're not too far from the coast here, and unlike in the interior, these are big, moist, warm blizzards that pile up deep snow very fast. We're stuck inside, reading and playing cards all day. This morning the stakes at cards was a box of peanuts. The loser had to go outside in the storm and get the nuts from our buried food cache up under the cornice. Ome lost—and he's the only man in camp who won't touch peanuts.

Finally around 9:15 it all cleared off. There's a cold, half moon floating through the skies above the rocky, black cliff behind camp. We may soon be able to sledge a load on up the valley to the upper cache that Ad and Jack supplied on the 4th. A trip way up the glacier to break trail will be necessary before we can push ahead after the next plane trip with our final supplies. The plane is due in four days.

SATURDAY, APRIL 13

We all went up the valley with the dogs and a load to the upper cache—some nine miles, we think—and broke the trail thoroughly all the way. We reached the cache after a stunning five-hour trip from Cascade Camp. We've given the name Bastion to a big peak that towers to an elevation of about 8,000 feet, right behind the cache. The gullies of Bastion were simply stupendous, clouds of fresh snow drifting off into the sky from their great black buttresses, and silvery clouds scudding by over the top in the deep blue.

The bulk of the east peak of Mount Hubbard seemed almost above me at the cache, but we still have a long way to go yet toward Mount Hubbard itself. Even to the corner must be another five or six miles. It's a long, long valley.

We returned to Cascade Camp, arriving back at five. The moon tonight is beautiful. It's almost like daylight outside. It will be grand for night work to have the moon in May. To bed at 8:45, comfortably tired after an eighteen-mile day.

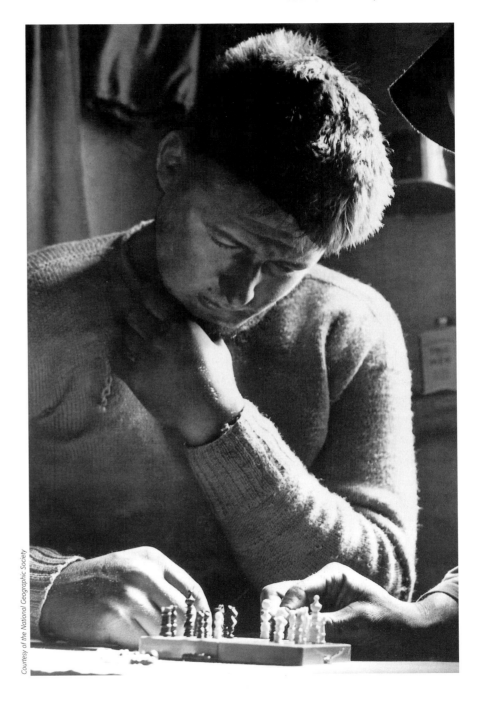

Courtesy of the National Geographic Society

Blizzards came often and furiously, and team members had to sit them out in tents or the small base-camp hut. Here, Ad Carter concentrates on a game of chess during one storm.

MONDAY, APRIL 15

While I was working on the map this morning, we heard a news report on the radio direct from Bordeaux, France. And this afternoon we heard the New York radio show *Amos and Andy* for the first time. We nearly split with laughter at them.

The radio reception is so good it seems as if we ought to get good weather before long and perhaps with it, the plane. The dogs don't seem to mind storms at all. They're curled up in the drifts sleeping peacefully. The other day Fanny got completely buried, and Cracker was buried completely except for one ear.

WEDNESDAY, APRIL 17

Bob, Jack, and I sledged and skied with the dogs and two days of food eight miles down the glacier to clean up the survey job on the lower end of our valley and leave a big cache down there for use on our way out at the end of the expedition.

While Jack made camp, Bob and I made a dandy set of survey observations. What a relief to see a sunset: One feels so free and light to be camped out on the flat again after weeks in the shadow of that great cliff beside the icefall. We plan to return to Cascade Camp at daybreak.

The dogs can pull like nothing human and seem to like it, so long as you go ahead of them. They race and bark and yelp and try to catch up for all they're worth, no matter how many miles they've gone, as long as there's more sledging ahead . . . and a good meal in the offing!

THURSDAY, APRIL 18

It took until past 9:30 to break camp and by noon, after working in what felt like stifling heat, we finally reached the station at which we'd surveyed some days earlier. After surveying, we raced back to Cascade Camp. On the map work, I noted the positions of our survey stations and have plotted all the peaks down both sides of the valley. What a swell feeling to get that job done.

SATURDAY, APRIL 20

We started out to move up the glacier with supplies for a new camp for four men, but as soon as all the dogs had been hitched up and the tent down and the mattresses let out, the clouds rolled in from the southwest and today went on the official record as another bad one. God knows how many.

We quickly decided to send Jack, Andy, and Bob down the side of the glacier opposite camp (we've taken to calling it the Dusty Glacier) to get fresh bear meat for the dogs and to put up a set of survey markers. They left with the dogs at noon and won't be back for at least four days.

SUNDAY, APRIL 21

Easter Sunday. We were peacefully awakened by the singing of the snowbirds. After we went to bed last night, the wind had blown like fury—but when we woke up, it was still and calm. My, but this country has its contrasts.

By midafternoon it was getting cool and the mists were blowing gently away. Great thunderheads lurked over the mountains toward Carcross. Spring must be arriving there. East Hubbard rose superb and ethereal, draped in silvery mantles of glistening fresh snow with feathery veils of mist drifting off. We surveyed from Cascade Station till nearly six o'clock, spellbound by the beauty of the scene.

MONDAY, APRIL 22

Shortly after we had cornmeal for breakfast, Ad cried out: "The plane!" We all rushed out of our tents. Strangely, this was the fourth time in a row that a sought-after plane had arrived while we'd been cooking cornmeal on an Alaska expedition. Cornmeal has magical properties, no doubt!

I slammed on my skis and reached the landing area just as Bob Randall finished taxiing. He delivered quite a pile of mail: I had telegrams from dad and mother, and also from the National Geographic. Bob also brought a set of prints of all the pictures we took on the Mount Logan flight of March 7.

After a thorough but hasty glance through the telegrams, we fitted the

Bob Bates pauses before climbing around a dramatic pinnacle in the Lowell Glacier Icefall.

Courtesy of the National Geographic Society

photographic door on the plane and took off for some aerial surveying and photography. We swung around the southern side of Mount Hubbard, then turned northward over the mass of unknown peaks east and north of Mount Vancouver. We ran through the pass between Mount Walsh and Mount Lucania, getting simply glorious pictures. I've never seen such a huge mass of immense glaciers.

We turned south again, up the valley of a great glacier that comes eastward from Mount Walsh. We passed one area of this glacier that heads up to the south of Walsh, and we continued to where it and the Kaskawulsh Glacier and the Hubbard Glacier merge in one great snowfield 8,000 or so feet high. A big snow mound, scarcely a mountain, really, which is at least 12,500 feet high, rises from this snowfield. We later named this peak Mount Queen Mary. We swung about this to the left, taking a picture of a peak that rises to 12,000 feet or so in a stupendous pinnacle of rock and ice, and we named this Mount King George. The peaks were named in honor of the British monarchs, marking the 25th anniversary—the silver jubilee—of King George V's accession to the throne. These are now known as the Jubilee Peaks.

It was noon as we turned in front of Mount St. Elias and took a series of pictures of that gigantic peak and the incredible wall of Mount Logan opposite it. Logan had put on its daily storm cap, but our pictures of it this morning were corkers. We reached camp after a closeup flight to inspect the cliffs of Hubbard and Alverstone.

After lunch back at Cascade Camp, we took off and flew down the Dusty Glacier over the trail of Jack, Andy, and Bob Bates. One could clearly follow it all the way to a camp on the moraine near its end 12 miles down near the Alsek River. Then we swung down the Alsek, having a look at Bates Lake and Kathleen Lake as prospective places where part of our party might be picked up in June. We decided on Bates Lake as the better option. We returned to camp, and at five o'clock, Bob Randall roared off for Carcross again.

Now we're to be alone here until June 3—no more airplane flights.

Courtesy of the National Geographic Society

Brad Washburn sights through the theodolite while Ad Carter takes notes during a surveying session from a rock ledge, a tiny island in an ocean of ice and snow.

Brad Washburn holds his large-format Fairchild F-8 camera, which he used to shoot all aerial photos during the Yukon expedition. With him is pilot Bob Randall.

Courtesy of the National Geographic Society

TUESDAY, APRIL 23

We made a major discovery at lunch. We found we could manufacture delectable peanut butter by running peanuts through the meat grinder and then frying them with butter, olive oil, bacon grease, and salt.

In the afternoon we looked over all of my aerial photos that Bob Randall had brought in to us, and I've been very carefully labeling all the peaks by number with ink to help us in surveying. It's still snowing—light, feathery flakes that seem to take hours to pile up any depth. There's not a breath of wind. You can walk along in the snow and not even feel it.

WEDNESDAY, APRIL 24

We're in the midst of another terrific southwester. You can't predict when you'll get a storm or have any idea of how long it will last. Our little house is shaking and quivering at every blast and the snow is coming by horizontally outside. The cook tent is almost completely out of sight.

The pictures are now all mounted and labeled neatly in an album that we can take everywhere when we survey. Now I'm tackling the altitude computations for all the peaks down the north side of our valley. Ome and I have been figuring out the names of some of the peaks along the Canada-Alaska boundary which have so far been pretty much of a mystery for us.

FRIDAY, APRIL 26

Up at six o'clock with the wind just screaming by camp. We decided to move camp up the icefall and start the siege on Mount Hubbard, even if it's cold in the wind.

The going has been terrible with powder snow, but we're pushing through this time if it's humanly possible. We hauled two loads up the hill this morning and one this afternoon. We tried to hand-sledge a bit up the valley this evening, but there was no use in all the powder, and we've camped here for the night at the top of the icefall at a glorious new temporary location.

The icefall pitches below us with all its seracs and crevasses now in the warmth of spring—then there are twenty glittering miles of white stretching

Courtesy of the National Geographic Society

Ad Carter and dogs negotiate a steep pitch of the Lowell Glacier icefall.

to the Alsek River. Above us leads the long trench of the glacier winding out of sight behind the vast black cliffs of Mount Bastion.

We plan to sledge to a camp at the upper cache if we can get a few more hours of decent weather. Here's praying for a little bit of good luck tomorrow.

BASTION CAMP ON LOWELL GLACIER
SATURDAY, APRIL 27, 1935

We fought our way to the upper cache (Bastion Camp) today through snow that was God-awful: breakable, windblown crust on top of a foot of loose, feathery powder. When we finally reached the campsite, Bob and I lay down to doze for thirty minutes before we dared to eat. Then we snapped up some sardines and slept some more before we put up the tent. The others, with the sledge, pulled in later, and after supper the weather cleared, giving us a cold north wind.

Refreshed, Harty and I left at 6:30 this evening and made a scouting trip further up the valley, making an eight-mile round-trip. Our destination at the foot of East Hubbard is some eight miles away, but we have a good trail and ought to make it tomorrow.

SUNDAY, APRIL 28

Up at five o'clock on a perfect day, and on the move up the valley at six. We discovered that a "shelf route" may exist up Mount Alverstone, or even Mount Hubbard. At any rate we hand-sledged for eight solid hours up the main Lowell Glacier and up the Avalanche Glacier, which is not half as badly crevassed as it appeared.

We finally reached an altitude of 8,000 feet at the very foot of the terrific 6,000-foot cliffs of East Hubbard, whence a tiny shelf leads to an upper shelf. We must do some very speedy climbing through there, as the landscape is dominated by seracs 4,000 to 5,000 feet above the route. What a stupendous sight. That great East Hubbard-Alverstone ridge is just steaming with powder snow.

The sledge enabled us to bring five days' worth of food with us to this point—the site at 8,000 feet of our final camp. We also have three 300-foot

ropes, a heavy manila rope, two 30-meter cotton ropes, a saw, an aerial camera, a movie camera, 350 feet of movie film, and other gear.

After unloading the sledge, we headed back to Bastion Camp for the night.

MONDAY, APRIL 29

Today Jack went down to Cascade Camp with the dogs for a last load of ice axes, crampons, rappel pickets, and miscellaneous other utensils we may need as we go upward. Andy and I spent the whole day surveying and occupied four nearby survey stations.

Then a grand supper of bear meat from a bear shot on the boys' recent foray down the Dusty Glacier valley. Boy, but it's good—Hubbard is being surveyed on bear meat. It certainly tastes good to eat something that's real chewy.

When we went to bed at nine there was a superb sunset without a cloud in the sky. We're sleeping four in our Logan tent and three in the cook tent. This mass sleeping is very warm and we're getting in some good snoozes. Everybody is in superb shape and we're ready for anything.

TUESDAY, APRIL 30

Up at 5:00 a.m. and sledged like dogs with the dogs all day till 4:30 p.m., finally reaching our final camp, at 8,000 feet, after some real exertion. We were toting a 400-pound load up really steep slopes on a hell of a hot day. We saw two terrific avalanches today. This is a stunning campsite.

We spent a rather fitful night on account of wild wind and blowing snow. I spent most of the night with a tent peg jamming me in the back. What a life.

WEDNESDAY, MAY 1

In the morning we had a magnificent view of East Hubbard, towering right above our tents. Harty, Jack, Ome, and I started off to scout the Shelf and make an effort to complete the surveying up there. Ome was so slow and the route necessitated such great speed that we absorbed his load and the three of us pushed ahead while he returned to camp.

Courtesy of the National Geographic Society

The ice-covered buttresses of Mount Bastion rise above camp on the upper Lowell Glacier, nine miles up from Cascade Camp.

The route up the Shelf is one of the most awe-inspiring climbs I've done in my life. For nearly a mile and a half it's overhung by seracs thousands of feet above—a huge, glittering wall ready to topple at a moment's notice. Or rather, with no notice at all. We pushed ahead at breakneck speed, but even then we took an hour and a half to get out of danger.

After a short rest at the beginning of the Shelf, or plateau, at 11,000 feet, we pushed ahead into a hard wind. It was a slow fight. It took us an hour and three-quarters to make the two and a half miles that put us abreast of Mount Alverstone. We ate lunch in a little col at 12,200 feet. Then we set up the theodolite a hundred feet east of the col on some snow-covered rocks and started what was one of the most frigid surveys I've ever attempted.

The wind came in terrific gusts, but we planted the tripod securely in the rocks, and the results always seemed to check out correctly. Blowing snow accompanied every gust—and the wind always jerked my eye from the telescope and made it difficult to read the figures. Without our aerial picture book we'd have been utterly lost. We located loads of new peaks, though the actual top of Mount Logan was in clouds. We were working from the highest survey station ever occupied in the Yukon Territory of Canada.

In midafternoon a sea of clouds rolled in from the ocean and up the Hubbard Glacier, and clouds began whirling wildly off the peak of Alverstone above us. We started to head back down. All day long we'd had a sinking feeling about having to descend beneath that section of overhanging seracs. An enormous avalanche had fallen just after we passed in the morning.

On the way down we prepared for a breakneck dash through this danger zone by throwing away our two ropes in order to lighten the load. Then we started off beneath those menacing seracs, running hell-bent for camp. We tripped over our snowshoes and ourselves a dozen times, swore, looked up at the towers of ice above us, and then brushed the snow out of our eyes and started off again. With dread in our hearts, we simply flew down the 2,700 feet to camp. Zeus, what a good feeling to be back, safe and sound in every limb, at the end of the single most important day of this expedition's survey program.

Courtesy of the National Geographic Society

The expedition's highest camp, at 8,300 feet, was set at the base of the great cliffs of East Hubbard—later named Mount Kennedy by the Canadian government in memory of the assassinated U.S. president.

65

THURSDAY, MAY 2

It was a cold, grey morning, with signs of an approaching storm hovering over Alverstone. Harty and I surveyed from a station just below camp before stopping for lunch. After lunch we all broke camp and headed back down. The most important job for us now is to complete our surveying. If we stayed to climb Alverstone or Hubbard, that would mean risking our lives and the more important work just for a stunt.

We put the whole camp on two sledges. Ad and Jack managed the dog sledge, and the rest of us took a thousand pounds on the other sledge. It was snowing lightly as we left the 8,000-foot campsite, but small spots of sunshine were still visible on the Lowell Glacier. About ninety minutes later we were safely back on the valley floor.

Our old Bastion Camp was in a thick storm as we progressed out onto the flat. At 5:30 we pulled up the small hill a mile from the camp, and there the storm hit us full force. Ad and Jack had hurried ahead and set up a tent. Zeus, those dogs can move!

We bucked a thirty-mile wind laden with driving, drifting snow. We'd fought on for twenty minutes when Jack and the dogs came rushing back out of the gale, the dogs pulling him on skis. The dogs hitched onto our load and pulled it into Bastion Camp at a trot, just as if it weighed nothing.

CASCADE CAMP ON LOWELL GLACIER
FRIDAY, MAY 3, 1935

The going was terrible today as we returned to Cascade Camp. Jack, Bob, and I traveled with a 400-pound sledge-load through snow that was deep, sticky, and fresh. The sled must have turned over a thousand times in the nine miles from Bastion Camp, and when we finally got home, Jack claimed it was the worst trail he'd ever mushed over. That's something. All praise to the dogs. They are magnificent.

Supper was fantastic. Cold tomato juice, bear-meat hamburgers, creamed corn, thick mushroom soup, and to cap it off, a juicy fig pudding. It's nice to

Courtesy of the National Geographic Society

Two climbers pause for a brief rest on May 1, 1935, tiny figures in a landscape dominated by East Hubbard (later named Mount Kennedy).

On the way down from their highest surveying station May 1, Brad Washburn and his companions rushed through this area, trying to avoid the frequent avalanches off these cliffs. Here, Jack Haydon stops to adjust a snowshoe binding. The huge west face of East Hubbard (Mount Kennedy) towers behind him.

Courtesy of the National Geographic Society

be back in our little hut again. It's so toasty warm and comfortable and springlike despite the big flakes still drifting by outside. If we get another stretch of good weather, we'll be able to begin making our way down to the ocean and Yakutat.

SATURDAY, MAY 4

Good weather? We got socked by a terrific snowstorm. The whole camp is drifted in like the dead of winter, and all feelings of spring fever are banished. In great contrast to what we were viewing, the radio picked up programs playing spring tunes and people talking of the flowers and the beauties of spring.

MONDAY, MAY 6

It was a cloudless morning except for a low sea of mists over the eastern hills. We were heading back up to Bastion Camp—Jack and his dogs to pick up a final load, and Harty and I to do more surveying. The dogs, each hitched in his harness, frolicked gaily all about us. It's marvelous how much excess energy they always seem to have.

We'd just reached the crest of the first steep pitch a hundred feet above camp when the six unharnessed dogs went tearing off to our right, leaping and playing, five of them chasing after the dog named Cracker. All of a sudden I saw one tail in the air, disappearing down through a narrow slit in the snow, and then there were only three dogs in sight. Jack rushed toward the spot and found himself at the very edge of a huge crevasse.

I yelled to him to watch out. We grabbed the three remaining dogs, who were whining and running around aimlessly about a tiny hole. Tex, Cracker, and Tip were all right. But Brownie, Fannie, and Monkey were nowhere to be seen. We ran over as near to the hole as we dared, then crawled on our hands and knees and peered in. We were leaning out over a vast crevasse with an almost completely snowed-over top.

Jack called out wildly, "Brownie! Brownie!" Not a sound came from below. The crevasse went straight down for thirty feet and then, amid a mass of jagged slices of ice, twisted toward us and went out of sight under us into the deep blue-green bowels of the glacier. We called again: "Fannie! Monkey!" Not a sound.

We yelled down to Bob Bates at camp to bring a rope. He picked up a hundred-foot coil and rushed up the 45-degree pitch as fast as his legs would carry him. We staked a pair of skis deeply in the snow at a safe distance from the edge of the hole and tied one end of the rope to the skis. I tied myself to the other end.

We let the loop of slack down into the hole, and I hitched up in "rappel" mode and slid over the edge of the snow through the narrow hole the dogs had made into the upper vault of the chasm. For the first twenty feet, the walls were hard-packed winter snow. Chunks of the lip of the crack kept falling on my head as I descended. The ice walls of the crevasse were covered with dog shit—those poor falling dogs were really "scared shitless!"

It was clear that the dogs must have glanced off the wall to my right and fallen far into a deep grotto that ran below me out of sight. I wedged myself crosswise, chimney-fashion, between the icy walls, and yelled for those above me to move the skis and rope over to my right by ten or twelve feet. There was much scuffling up above and lots of snow fell down my neck.

I couldn't hear a sound. I've never known a more hopeless feeling than to be jammed thirty feet below the surface in a cold, clammy crevasse, with a loose, useless rope dangling from above. Then a reassuring yell came. They'd had to smash open a new hole above me through which to pass the rope, and that had caused all the snowfall. The rope tightened and I started on down again.

The light grew dimmer as I slid down under the overhang. Far below me in the greyness, I saw something move. Splotches of blood stained the ice walls beside me. I called, "Monkey!" No reply, but a faint movement was visible. As my eyes adjusted to the dim light, I could see all three dogs lying on top of each other. Fannie was on the bottom, Brownie was next, and Monkey was on top. They were huddled in a shivering mass atop a heap of shattered ice.

They were still thirty feet below me and I didn't dare move an inch further until I'd pulled off a huge, loose chunk of ice that was clinging by God-knows-what to the wall just beneath me, and would surely be knocked

Courtesy of the National Geographic Society

The six dogs that accompanied the expedition proved their worth time and again, eagerly hauling loads on the Lowell Glacier.

off onto either the dogs or me. Bracing myself securely, I pulled off the chunk and tossed it down a chasm beyond the dogs. It clattered from wall to wall and then crashed far below us in the dark depths.

The rope wasn't nearly long enough to reach the dogs. After I'd waited what seemed like an age, jammed crosswise once more, I received a second hundred-foot rope. With the new rope, I speedily made the final descent. It was no place to linger, with tons of loose blocks of ice hanging just above me, ready to fall at the slightest movement of the glacier. I quickly slipped a noose of the new rope through the harness of each dog, then I called out, "OK!" Then I was hauled up—nine-tenths by those above, one-tenth by myself—on the fixed rope.

As we began, I saw Monkey giving me one last pitiful glance. Then I was out of sight, being pulled into the upper grotto and finally crawling out over the lip of the crevasse and into the beautiful, warm sunlight of that early May morning.

We started to haul the dogs out, but soon after we began lifting them, there was a little jerk and the load lightened a lot. The implication was clear. One of the harnesses must have broken. Which one was it? And how far had that dog fallen? In a jiffy, the little forms of two dogs came over the edge of the crevasse and we dragged Fannie and Brownie out onto the loose snow, to safety. They were terrified to the point of utter stillness and shivered all over with cold and fright. But what about poor Monkey?

I had had all I wanted of that crevasse, so Ad Carter went down. He found the dog, and soon Ad was back up. Then Monkey was pulled up, bedraggled, but still alive. I will never understand to my dying day how those dogs could fall at least seventy feet through that maze of jagged, torn ice and come out with no more injury than two cut lips (Brownie and Monkey) and one lost toenail (Monkey).

Now, after a cold, windy, cloudy day, it's cleared off and we've had a beautiful, pink sunset. It's great to have everything ready for the trip to the coast. We've sorted out all of our food and we have thirty-five days' worth left. It's uncertain just how long it will take us to finish the ski movies we want to make, to wrap up the surveying, and to make it to the sea.

TUESDAY, MAY 7

Jack took the dogs and a load of gas, food, and other gear and began heading toward our new campsite on the route down toward the coast and Yakutat. The rest of us spent the morning packing up Cascade Camp, and now we're ready to move the whole outfit at the slightest streak of favorable weather.

EN ROUTE TO YAKUTAT

WEDNESDAY, MAY 8, 1935

Perfect and cloudless. We left Cascade Camp and dog-sledged two loads and hand-sledged one huge load to our old camp down the glacier. I was grateful for an Ovaltine reviver before bed. We're at last on our way to Yakutat.

THURSDAY, MAY 9

The morning mist burned off into pleasant, warm sunlight that permitted me to make my final observations on the nearby peaks. What a beautiful camp this was. The magnificent glacier leading westward past Mount Hubbard was lined with a stupendous array of mountains, a full dozen of them rising higher than 10,000 feet and none of them ever seen before.

We sledged six hundred pounds as far as we could pull it over terrible, brittle crust in a blazing sun. In the evening, after making camp, Harty and I made a six-mile exploratory trip downward toward our goal, Yakutat. At last we sniffed a real sea smell, borne on the gentle wings of a soft, southerly breeze.

FRIDAY, MAY 10

We moved camp down to the flat area near where Harty and I explored last night. There are loads of sparrows, chickadees, and juncos here. It seems quite like home in Boston to hear them chirping outside.

SATURDAY, MAY 11

The damned clouds descended again and a stiff, cool wind and a driving snowstorm started. We were so furious at being thwarted in our plans to do surveying that we shouldered the theodolite and tripod, the extra tent, a tent pole, a big survey marker, and lunch and started down anyway. But we were back at camp again in the afternoon amid a thick, drifting blizzard. There just doesn't seem to be any end to this filthy weather, which, as expected, gets worse and worse as we near the coast.

SUNDAY, MAY 12

Our new "waterproof" tents that were to be so strong that they could stand any wind are leaking like old sieves and have had to be mended in a dozen places. Little pools of water are collecting on the floor, and all our clothes are getting slowly soaked. We've punched holes in the floor to let the water drain out. I am from New England, but honest to God, I have never seen such a hell's kitchen for weather in my life.

TUESDAY, MAY 14

Another night of anguish! Andy got up at midnight and I got up at 5:30. Nothing doing: all mist and fog in every direction, except toward our old Cascade Camp.

This morning we had a vital council of war on our final plans. We've decided to split up instead of trying to bring all seven men and the dogs down the unknown route to Yakutat. So we have arranged our plan as follows: that we all stick together until about May 20; then Jack and the dogs will stay with Andy, Harty, and me for a while longer, transporting thirty days of food, while Ad, Ome, and Bob start a trek to Bates Lake, where we hope they'll be picked up by a plane. Jack and the dogs will then race to join them. After Ome and Ad fly to Carcross, they will wire Yakutat for a boat to meet us at the foot of the glacier. Bob and Jack will mush on to Kluane and meet us later. We feel that our expedition should separate into two parties so that if we run into real trouble, at least one party is sure to get to safety and then, somehow, help the other.

We surveyed all day from the point we called the Mound in a bitterly raw southeast wind. We didn't complete the job, or even see the southerly boundary peaks at all, but we did clean up survey work on dozens of tiny peaks.

Final Glacier
Camp

Hell's
Half
Mile

Tidewater
Camp

Nunatak
Fiord

Courtesy of the National Geographic Society

Four members of the Yukon expedition team negotiated the treacherous edge of this glacier to reach tidewater at Nunatak Fiord. With the glacier too crevassed for safe travel and the adjoining cliffs too steep to climb, they were forced along a narrow corridor where they were pelted with rocks falling from the slopes above—along a route they called Hell's Half Mile.

Courtesy of the National Geographic Society

THURSDAY, MAY 16

We broke camp, leaving with an immense hand-sledge load. The going was rottener and rottener all the way. We made twelve miles to our next camp.

FRIDAY, MAY 17

A glorious, cloudless day after the morning mist wilted away. Jack and I went ahead, I on skis and Jack with a dog-team load. We took lovely movies all the way and reached the top of the last low pass between us and tidewater at 9:40. Mount Vancouver and our two new peaks, Mounts King George and Queen Mary, were magnificent in the morning shadows, way up the Hubbard Glacier (named after Gardiner Greene Hubbard, first president of the National Geographic Society).

Ome, Andy, Bob, and Harty sledged a big load and arrived a little more than an hour behind us. But they forgot lunch! We had no water at all in any form. We rifled a food sack and guzzled a can of caviar in triumph—right on the crest of this final pass.

After lunch we all climbed a hill behind the pass (to an elevation of 6,000 feet). The route to Yakutat looks grand. Jack and I put in two hellish hours in the glaring sun and surveyed every new peak we've seen, as well as the two summits of Mount Vancouver. We certainly have a wealth of new knowledge about this huge St. Elias Range.

Returning to camp thoroughly tired and sunburned, we discovered that the cook tent had burned up completely. The pole went up through the roof just after Andy came back. He got his hair singed and managed to save everything except my sleeping bag and Duxbak jacket and three pairs of socks. I guess we'll have to beat it for Yakutat posthaste now.

Andy smokes continually. A half-extinguished cigarette must have led to this conflagration.

The Yukon expedition named this 12,300-foot peak Mount King George, in honor of the 25th anniversary of his accession to the British throne—and Queen Mary was honored in the naming of a nearby 13,000-foot mountain.

SATURDAY, MAY 18

Andy and I fought our way back up to the final pass, sledging 350 pounds. Jack started with the dogs two hours later. We've got an overnight camp pitched on the south side of the pass and about a half-mile down from the top, on the Art Lewis Glacier. While we were starting lunch, Ad pulled in. He will be traveling with us to Yakutat, after all. Harty arrived later.

After supper, Harty, Ad, and I took a 600-pound sledge load down the hill in the cool of the evening and wound our way safely onto the floor of the Art Lewis Glacier, leaving the load at a cache site before returning back up to our camp. All we need now is a good day tomorrow and a good route to the water.

The twilight shadows stretched across the narrow valley, and soft grey mists floated in from the sea. We could see the sunlight on the left valley wall twelve miles away, where it was pouring in from the ocean. How soft and pleasant the air seemed, wafted upward from those mysterious depths that hold the last secret of the expedition.

SUNDAY, MAY 19

Jack hitched the dogs onto his empty sledge, and after fond and almost tearful farewells we bade him and all the dogs goodbye. Then they left for Cascade Camp to join Bob and Ome for the trek down Lowell Glacier to the Alsek River, which they planned to cross by raft before hiking on to Bates Lake. For us, it's now downhill all the way to the coast.

We traveled as far as we could in the morning until the crust began breaking under the weight of our sledge, and it became impossible to move the load through the slush. We set up camp in a stiff cross-glacier breeze at 3,500 feet. The breeze got steadily worse until a storm was on us full blast. Rain came down in sheets and, combined with the wind, it felt as if it would tear our tent to shreds. The driving snow and rain were whipped along so hard by the wind that a fine, steady rain fell inside the tent.

Ad thinks that the directors of the Woods Company, which made this tent, should be put in it in a wind tunnel and have tests made with an eighty-mile

Courtesy of the National Geographic Society

Only ten miles from tidewater at the end of the expedition, team members were stopped by a three-day blizzard that buried their camp under 100 inches of wet snow.

gale plus at least 90 percent water, at 38 degrees. There ought to be a rule that all tents must be slept in by those who claim they're waterproof, before they're sold to the public.

MONDAY, MAY 20

Everything is soaked and dripping. It snowed more than a foot of soft, wet slush all over everything last night. It seems a curious bit of luck that we should be fated to sit here, less than ten miles from tidewater, for several days without ever seeing our goal. It will be a real feat to cross this damnable range if we finally can!

TUESDAY, MAY 21

It's all we can do to keep the tent shoveled out. We have food left for about twelve days or so, so I guess we're all right for a while.

We have been packing a small inflatable boat with us, and our plan is to use it after we reach the foot of the glacier at Nunatak Fiord. Andy and I hope to paddle the final distance to the cannery at Yakutat in this six-foot-long boat and then return in a motorboat to get Ad and Harty.

WEDNESDAY, MAY 22

It has now snowed without a break for seventy-three hours.

THURSDAY, MAY 23

Hurrah, the great storm is over! It's really cold and there is a good crust on the snow. If the rotten clouds will stay where they are now for twelve hours, Andy and I may very soon be on our way to Yakutat.

I wonder what the lower end of the glacier will bring us. We're worried that it may end in a high, vertical ice cliff. From our aerial photos, we know that the last mile of this glacier is impassable because of the great concentration of big crevasses. We also know that the steep valley wall that will be on our right is unclimbable. But we're counting on lots of hard, windpacked snow between the crevasses and the wall to offer us a safe route to tidewater.

FRIDAY, MAY 24

It would take a year to write down half of what's happened since daybreak today, as I lie here, curled up in a comfortable pair of light Fiala sleeping bags, on a tiny rock ledge about twenty feet above the waters of Nunatak Fiord—looking up at the magnificent ice front of the Nunatak Glacier. Every minute, it seems, enormous chunks of ice crash off into the water and thunder away, with mountains of spray. The bay is so clogged with icebergs that we wouldn't be able to get through, even with a tugboat—and the waves set off by the crashing ice are so huge that we couldn't think of trying to launch our rubber yacht yet.

We left our "blizzard camp" at 4:30 this morning, after a 2:00 a.m. reveille, and sledged a huge load to a campsite on a shelf of dry land, situated at the corner of the Art Lewis Glacier. It will be the camp where Ad and Harty will wait while Andy and I paddle on to Yakutat.

From the campsite, Ad and I went quite a bit ahead to investigate the route. I've never in my life been more worried, scared, or nervous than I have been all day long. The last half of our route to the ledge above Nunatak Fiord was as near a hell of worry, wondering, and real praying as I've ever known: places where the ice and bedrock met with big cliffs rising above us, smooth and unclimbable; places where we traversed waterfalls and brooks and soaked ourselves to the skin; places where it looked as if there would be a rock and ice cliff at the end of the glacier that we'd never be able to get down. We'd taken a long chance, betting on this route from airplane pictures, but I'm horribly afraid that all exploration is full of risks taken, as well as occasional failures.

As we reconnoitred the last part of this tortuous route, we had to thread our way through a constant barrage of little snow avalanches and rocks as big as a fist, falling from the cliffs to our right. As we neared the waters of Nunatak Fiord, this bombardment became worse as the sun rose higher and higher, melting more debris free from the slopes above us.

We found a route leading to this ledge at tidewater, where we are now camped. Andy and Harty descended it after us—all of us extremely happy to safely reach the end of what we're calling "Hell's Half Mile." Ad and Harty

Courtesy of the National Geographic Society

Ad Carter, Harty Beardsley, and Andy Taylor are silhouetted against Nunatak Fiord at the tidewater camp on May 24.

then returned to their campsite back at the corner of the Art Lewis Glacier.

Now our only opponents are the icepack and the wind. If we can just paddle that first half mile, then the ice won't bother us any more, nor the waves either. We've been camped on snow and ice for eighty days, and it's a thrill to be on dry land at last.

As I was getting our sleeping gear arranged and Andy was cooking a can of roast beef hash, I asked: "Andy, were you scared this afternoon?" His reply: "During the last half hour, the shit was right up in the back of my throat!" I've heard of people being scared shitless, but never before had I heard anything like Andy's memorable response.

SATURDAY, MAY 25

It was a short night. We got up at 2:00 a.m. when I spied the first break in the pack ice that had jam-packed the fiord from the moment of our arrival. We had a speedy breakfast of cornmeal mush, bacon, and coffee. But no sooner were we ready to launch our tiny boat than half the front of the glacier crashed off in a terrific poop and made the most complete ice jam you've ever seen— at least half a mile wide and extending down this side of the fiord as far as the eye could reach. Smaller pieces have been falling ever since, ranging in size from a peanut to a two-story office building—falling off the top, bursting out of the middle, or exploding up from beneath the water with terrific tidal waves.

We finally managed to shove off through a corner of this icepack. We took a chance, but we got away with it. Not thirty seconds after we'd managed to push through 100 feet of cracked ice and get into free water away from the cliffs, one of the most enormous hunks of ice yet broke off the glacier-front not 200 yards from where we'd launched the boat.

We made good speed, with a fine breeze behind us. In an hour the glacier disappeared from view and bits of vegetation began to appear on the barren valley walls. We ate a late lunch with hot tea and fresh water on a little gravel slope beside a tiny brook. After a two-hour rest, we started off again and paddled westward for three more hours till we finally pulled in on a beautiful, sandy beach, with real trees and a freshwater brook. Pure heaven!

SUNDAY, MAY 26

We woke up at six o'clock this morning to the tune of millions of songbirds and the constant clucking of a ptarmigan sitting right behind our lean-to. The bay was calm as glass, but the mountains were becoming buried in mist. Although the easiest way to the cannery at Yakutat would be to paddle north up Russell Fiord, past the face of the Hubbard Glacier, and then south through Disenchantment Bay, we were nervous about the big icebergs that always fall off the end of the Hubbard. So we decided to play the game safely and detour southward, down Russell Fiord—even though it will mean portaging several miles from the fiord over to Yakutat Bay.

We sped through breakfast and were off and on our way at 8:10. By late afternoon it started to rain and blow so hard that we holed up in a shoreside bivouac right opposite Mount Pinta. Andy made a wonderful fire while I cooked supper and, despite the rain, we're all dried out and ready for the night under a lean-to made with a tarp and our upside-down boat.

MONDAY, MAY 27

It's 8:30 p.m. and almost pitch dark in a thick spruce forest, bordering on a swamp just south of the Tebenkof hills. The cool, damp evening mists are rising from the swamp and there's a glorious evening choir of veeries and thrushes. Russell Fiord is now well behind us and we are under way with the portage across to Yakutat Bay.

Right after breakfast, we fought our way up a very steep pitch right behind last night's camp. It was nothing but mud, slushy snow, "devil's club," and God-awful alder bushes—all at an angle of at least 40 degrees, in the boiling sun. We knew that this slope led eventually to a good-sized lake that was on the map, or we'd never have climbed it. We are indeed now on a *real* map.

Once up the hill, we descended through the forest on the other side, Andy with a load of fifty pounds and I with at least ninety (after all, he's sixty years old and I'm not quite twenty-five). After wading down a brook bed and cursing at more devil's club and alders for two or three miles, we reached the lake.

We reinflated the boat and paddled down the lake—much better than

Courtesy of the National Geographic Society

Andy Taylor paddles the inflatable rubber boat that he and Brad Washburn used in traveling to their final destination at the cannery town of Yakutat, Alaska. Glacier ice floats behind him.

Courtesy of the National Geographic Society

Andy Taylor stands beside the "tent" that he and Brad Washburn used during their five-day trip from Nunatak Fiord to Yakutat: a tarp, and their rubber boat turned upside down.

bushwhacking. We then deflated the boat and continued southwestward through the forest for a little over two hours, toward a really large lake that was also on the map. But we never found that lake. We finally made camp on a slight hillside, which looks as if it's only about six miles from Yakutat Bay.

Quite a day! Fourteen hours on the trail, millions (no, billions) of mosquitoes, and huge packs. We've got to continue to carry that damned boat, as it's the only way we're finally going to get to Yakutat.

TUESDAY, MAY 28

Up early after a short night. The godsend of the day was a dandy footpath that we picked up near our camp. We lunched on it at noon, and we were then only about three miles from an inlet off Yakutat Bay. But it took us nearly seven hours to cover those last three miles.

We literally fought our way through bogs and windfalls, hills and hollows. We lost the trail shortly after lunch and continued in the bottom of a small creek, which soon filled up with more devil's club and alders. When we climbed a tree, it looked as if we had only a mile to go, but that mile never seemed to end. At seven o'clock, we picked up a real footpath and then, all of a sudden, we broke out of the woods and there was a wonderful little white cottage with green blinds, right in front of us on a wee island less than a mile away.

We blew up our trusty boat and paddled out to the island and its tempting little house. Nobody was home, but we appropriated its woodshed and have a fire going. There's lots of fresh rainwater in a hogshead and we have coffee brewing. The Pacific swells are rolling in on the beach, and it's thrilling to have a sheet-iron roof over our heads.

YAKUTAT, ALASKA
WEDNESDAY, MAY 29, 1935

The sea was glassy calm as we paddled triumphantly down Yakutat Bay, past one point and island after another. The vast mass of the Malaspina Glacier stretched far to our right, at the foot of the great cone of 18,000-foot Mount St. Elias.

Courtesy of the National Geographic Society

Brad Washburn packs a 90-pound load during the two-day portage of the rubber boat and other gear through thick forest, underbrush, and bogs to Yakutat Bay.

We lunched at an abandoned fox farm on Otmeloi Island, eight miles from where we started this morning—with only seven miles more to Yakutat. After lunch it began to blow hard, a headwind, but we buttoned up our jackets, pulled tarps over our knees, and pushed ahead. At two o'clock we sighted a fishing boat and at 2:45 we rounded the last point—and there was the cannery at Yakutat.

As we landed on a nice, sandy beach, the next wave swamped our tiny boat and filled it with saltwater. Several kids came rushing down to greet us. When they asked where on earth we'd come from, our unexpected response was "from Carcross, Yukon, Canada." The great St. Elias Range has been officially crossed!

THURSDAY, MAY 30

Yakutat! As soon as we arrived, Andy engaged a boat to go down Disenchantment Bay and Nunatak Fiord to pick up Ad and Harty back at the glacier and bring them out here to Yakutat. I went straight to the cannery's radio shack and began to send seemingly scores of messages telling our families and friends that we're at last safely back in civilization. I also sent a telegram to King George V of England, saying that we were proud to announce the naming of two great, hitherto unexplored peaks in honor of his jubilee year.

FRIDAY, MAY 31

While Andy was off picking up the boys at Nunatak Glacier, I was in the radio shack, receiving lots of congratulations from families and friends. All of a sudden the radio operator shoved back his chair and cried out: "Jesus Christ, this message is from the king!"

The message was signed by the British foreign secretary, and here's what it said:

"The King commands me to express to you the sincere appreciation of the compliment which the National Geographic Society Yukon Expedition have paid to his Majesty and to the Queen in naming two newly-discovered peaks after their majesties in commemoration of his silver jubilee. The King congratulates the expedition on their important achievement effecting the first crossing the Saint Elias Range from Yukon to Alaska."

Just as I was heading for bed, a fellow rushed to our little cabin to report that Andy's boat was already back from the glacier, with Ad and Harty and all of our stuff. I piled into my clothes, rushed down to the dock, and found that everything and everybody are OK. Ad and Harty will fly down to Juneau with us and take a boat direct to Seattle from there.

That's the end of the first of my two big worries—but my last and biggest one is to somehow fly from Juneau to Carcross and get Bob, Ome, Jack, and those dogs out from Bates Lake. We're hoping that Bob Randall has by now got his airplane on pontoons, so that we can speedily fly in and get them back to civilization.

SATURDAY, JUNE 1

We spent a rainy morning packing our supplies, getting ready to leave Yakutat, and at one o'clock the plane that we had radioed for pulled in. Now all of us are safely in Juneau after a magnificent flight down the coast, past Mount Fairweather, Lituya Bay, and Mount Crillon, our beloved friends of last year. But no sooner had we hit Juneau than we received a telegram from Carcross saying that Bates Lake is still frozen solid and that there's no way to land there. We've now got to hustle up to Carcross and drop food for the boys till we can land and get them out.

SUNDAY, JUNE 2

Andy and I couldn't take off for Carcross till one o'clock because of the usual lousy weather just north of Juneau. However, the skies slowly cleared off and we flew northward in a seaplane up Lynn Canal between two cloud layers. White Pass was buried in a dense sea of fog, but we managed to fly over it. Lake Bennett is still frozen solid, so we set down in the river on the other side of Carcross. Andy gathered up all of our unneeded gear that was left here during the winter and headed southward to Juneau and home on the afternoon plane.

Courtesy of the National Geographic Society

The end of the line for Brad Washburn and Andy Taylor in their inflatable boat was the tiny, sandy beach just to the right of the cannery at Yakutat, Alaska.

Courtesy of the National Geographic Society

Four members of the Yukon expedition ended the trip at the coastal community of Yakutat. They are (from left) Andy Taylor, Brad Washburn, Ad Carter, and Harty Beardsley.

Courtesy of the National Geographic Society

Three members of the Yukon party trekked out to Bates Lake, Yukon Territory, at the end of the expedition. They are (from left) Ome Daiber, Bob Bates, and Jack Haydon.

MONDAY, JUNE 3

Spent last night in Lynn Staples' cabin to avoid more hotel bills. I plan to spend tonight on Bob Randall's floor. It's been a glorious day here, all day long, but cloudy and squally over the mountains. We devoted the whole morning to putting the Fokker onto floats, as I'm determined to get food out to the boys at Bates Lake at the first possible chance.

At four o'clock, pilot Everett Wasson and I took off for Bates Lake—which turned out to be absolutely the only lake west of Carcross that was still covered with solid ice.

Since we couldn't land, we zoomed low over the boys' camp and dropped them lots of sacks of supplies: 30-30 cartridges, fishline and hooks, matches, butter, rice, bacon, Cream of Wheat, oatmeal, cornmeal, salt, sugar, coffee, cans of milk, cheese, tea bags, macaroni, prunes, beans, and pilot crackers. We did our work and beat it back to Carcross, as a storm from the north was rushing down on us.

THURSDAY, JUNE 6

Still waiting for Bates Lake to thaw out. A wonderful telegram arrived today from Dr. Gilbert Grosvenor, president of the National Geographic Society. It said, in part: "Heartiest congratulations to you and to every member of your courageous and resourceful group. Your successful accomplishment of extremely difficult explorations as originally planned reflect greatest credit on every individual in your party." We plan to make another four o'clock flight to Bates Lake tomorrow in the cold early-morning air.

FRIDAY, JUNE 7

My 25th birthday, with a glorious, cloudless morning. Up at 3:10 a.m. Breakfasted at dawn and went down to the Fokker, but Everett Wasson wasn't there. At his house I discovered that he is sick and cannot fly. What a terrible disappointment on a marvelous day. I wired pilot Frank Barr at nearby Atlin, and to my amazement he suddenly landed at Carcross in his tiny Stinson monoplane. We were on our way at about eleven o'clock.

It was gorgeous weather all the way. Mount Fairweather seemed but a stone's throw away as did Mount Hubbard, Mount Logan, and the other peaks on the boundary between the Yukon and Alaska. Bates Lake remained still mostly covered with ice, but a large patch of open water right near the boys' camp at last made possible a safe landing.

The fellows were all in camp, waving wildly. We didn't have enough fuel to relay all three of them back to Carcross in Frank Barr's little airplane, so we moved them over to the nearby northern end of big Dezadeash Lake in two relays. There they are on the Kluskhu Trail, along which they can easily reach the town of Champagne in a couple of days afoot, and then they can get to Whitehorse by truck, then on to Carcross by train. Bob, Jack, and the dogs are now doing this. Ome was not in as good a shape as Bob and Jack, so he flew back to Whitehorse with me and Frank.

It's a grand and glorious feeling to have all of my team back to safety at last. It will be several more days before Bob and Jack arrive, so I'll wait for them here in Whitehorse. But the National Geographic's Yukon Expedition has at last come to a triumphant end.

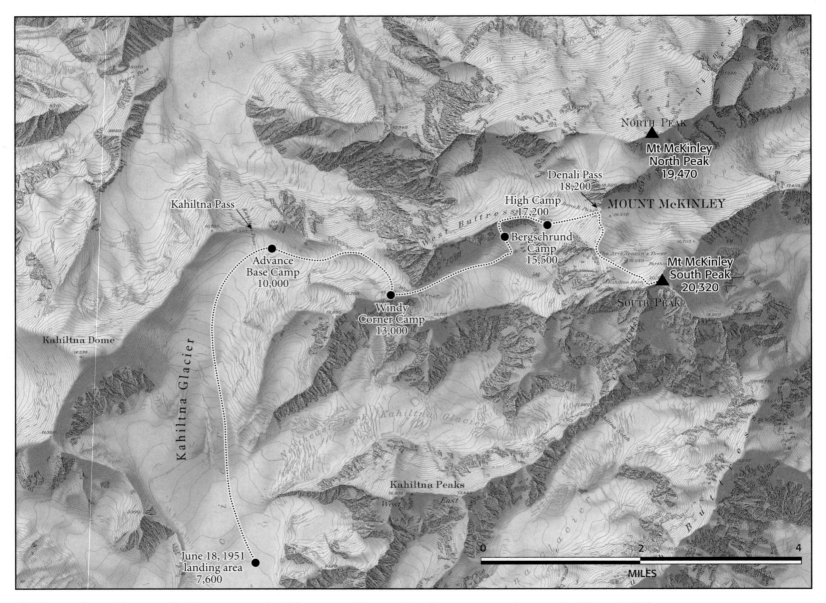

Kahiltna Pass

North Peak

Mt McKinley
North Peak
19,470

Denali Pass
18,200

High Camp
17,200

MOUNT McKINLEY

Bergschrund
Camp
15,500

Mt McKinley
South Peak
20,320

South Peak

Advance
Base Camp
10,000

Windy
Corner Camp
13,000

West Buttress

Kahiltna Dome

Kahiltna Glacier

Northeast Fork Kahiltna Glacier

Kahiltna Peaks
West   East

June 18, 1951
landing area
7,600

0   2   4

MILES

All eight members of the 1951 climbing team completed the ascent of the new West Buttress route to the summit of Mount McKinley.
Beginning on the Kahiltna Glacier, the route travels over Kahiltna Pass, thence to Windy Corner, up the West Buttress, and then to
Denali Pass and the summit. *Map surveyed and edited by Bradford Washburn.*

MOUNT McKINLEY
FIRST ASCENT OF THE WEST BUTTRESS

1951

To Jim Gale, a magnificent partner on any great mountain.

THROUGH HIS THREE PIONEERING ASCENTS of Mount McKinley and his creation of the definitive map of the mountain, Bradford Washburn became the man most identified with the hemisphere's most sought-after peak. He made his first climb of the mountain in 1942 as part of a U.S. Army group testing cold-weather equipment. The climb marked only the third ascent of the mountain, highest in North America.

He returned in 1947 for another climb, and it was on this trip that his wife, Barbara, became the first woman to reach the summit. Both climbs followed the original Muldrow Glacier route, from the northeast.

The origins of the 1951 first ascent of the West Buttress go back to the 1947 climb, when a scientist from the University of Chicago accompanied the Washburn party in order to conduct high-altitude cosmic ray studies for the Office of Naval Research. The scientist, Hugo Victoreen, carried out the experiments at an elevation of 18,200 feet at Denali Pass.

The Office of Naval Research later asked Washburn if he could find a shorter, easier, and safer way to reach Denali Pass. He eventually proposed a ski-plane landing on the Kahiltna Glacier followed by a climb of the West Buttress.

Washburn then learned that a team from Denver was planning to attempt the West Buttress in the late spring of 1951. He telephoned team leader Henry Buchtel and asked if he, Jim Gale, and Bill Hackett—all veterans of the 1947 climb—could join forces with him. Buchtel agreed.

Scientific inquiry was a primary goal of the 1951 expedition. Four men in Buchtel's party traveled by pack train overland to the Kahiltna Glacier from Wonder Lake, conducting geological studies on the way, while the other expedition members led by Washburn worked on surveying. Then all eight men turned their attention to climbing the West Buttress route.

The West Buttress climb was a fine mountaineering achievement, but by 1953 it no longer interested the Office of Naval Research. By then the agency had the use of powerful instruments that could do superior cosmic ray research without the need to go to high altitude.

Little did Washburn realize that the West Buttress ascent would help turn a 20,320-foot mountain into a kind of vacation getaway. By the 1990s, more than a thousand people a year were attempting to climb McKinley. All but a tiny percentage of the climbers use the West Buttress.

Four members of the eight-member 1951 Mount McKinley West Buttress team stand with pilot Terry Moore at the 7,600-foot expedition base camp on the Kahiltna Glacier. Pictured are (left to right) Moore, Henry Buchtel, Brad Washburn, Bill Hackett, and Jim Gale. Also on the team were John Ambler, Barry Bishop, Mel Griffiths, and Jerry More.

MOUNT MCKINLEY
FIRST ASCENT OF THE WEST BUTTRESS, 1951

Bradford (Brad) Washburn (leader), of Cambridge, Massachusetts

Dr. John Ambler, of Denver, Colorado

Barry Bishop, of Cincinnati, Ohio

Dr. Henry Buchtel, of Denver, Colorado

Sgt. James (Jim) Gale, U.S. Air Force, of Anchorage, Alaska

Professor Thomas Melvin (Mel) Griffiths, of Denver, Colorado

Capt. William (Bill) D. Hackett, U.S. Army, of Portland, Oregon

Jerry More, of Denver, Colorado

Pilot: Dr. Terris (Terry) Moore, President, University of Alaska

TO ALASKA

MAY 16-24, 1951

Off to Alaska at last after a month of feverish preparations. I traveled by plane from Boston to New York to Chicago to Denver to Seattle to Fairbanks.

Our equipment problems seem well in hand, but we still don't know if an Army helicopter will land Bill Hackett, Jim Gale, and me on the Kahiltna Glacier. If this works out, we'll establish base camp well in advance of the arrival of the team from Denver, who will come by pack train from the Wonder Lake area toward the end of June.

Received honorary PhD at the University of Alaska, in Fairbanks. Spoke at commencement. My speech was relatively brief—on the role of mountains in Alaskan science.

Concluded our packing during the next few days and gave a public lecture at the college. In the crowd were Charlie McGonagall, one of the original Sourdoughs who climbed McKinley's North Peak (19,470 feet) in 1910, and also Harry Karstens, who was in the first party to reach the summit of McKinley's South Peak (20,320 feet), on June 7, 1913. It may be the last time that he and Charlie stand before an audience together. Charlie is eighty-two.

Took the train to Nenana and then went on to McKinley Park.

MAY 27-29

Occupied several survey stations in the Broad Pass area, which are related to our new map of Mount McKinley. Especially good results from the summit of the Indian mountain, an important U.S. Geological Survey point near Chulitna Pass. It's located only about forty miles north of McKinley. Superb weather and very precise sights.

FRIDAY, JUNE 1

I've moved south to the Curry Hotel and station. Terry Moore wires that he is coming down here from the University of Alaska in Fairbanks and will spend the weekend with me. He plans to fly over and attempt a landing on the Kahiltna Glacier. My, how wonderful it would be if he could do that.

SATURDAY, JUNE 2

Terry Moore landed at the tiny local airstrip at eleven last night and we were off at 6:10 a.m. for McKinley. It was clouding up fast and though McKinley's summit was visible, it was all grey sky behind it. We were over Curry Lookout in five minutes; then we flew across the Chulitna River, over the very spot where Belmore Browne, Herschel Parker, and Merl La Voy camped in 1912 on their way to attempt the still-virgin summit of McKinley.

We swung up a dramatic valley just north of the Ruth Glacier, over a snow pass that led us to famous Glacier Point. Clouds were forming rapidly as we climbed through the incredible Great Gorge, its massive granite precipices towering far above us on both sides. As we emerged from the gorge and swung left over the 5,000-foot Ruth Amphitheater, we climbed through a layer

of ground fog and then headed up the southwest fork of the Ruth Glacier. Mount Silverthrone faded from view behind us, and the summit of McKinley—rapidly disappearing in menacing weather—now towered 10,000 feet above our airplane. Our flight up that icy canyon south of McKinley was the most dramatic flight I've ever made in Alaska.

The fantastic ice and rock slopes of the Rooster Comb, Mount Huntington, and McKinley were savage and impressive beyond description. Terry's little plane is so slow that we could easily circle at 60 mph within the confines of this amazing valley. We climbed slowly to 12,000 feet, then crossed the 11,000-foot pass between Mount Hunter and McKinley's South Buttress, and emerged at last over the broad valley of the Kahiltna Glacier. But, alas, the spot where we had hoped to land was deeply shrouded in fog. So we proceeded over Kahiltna Pass to try a landing in the upper basin of Peters Glacier.

The weather was all clear over the Peters, and we landed on perfect, dry snow with scarcely a bump: altitude 7,750 feet. No human being had ever landed where we now stood. There was a slight southwest breeze. We were thrilled at the tremendous face of Wickersham Wall that now towered nearly 12,000 feet above us to the top of McKinley's North Peak.

I hope that we can use this little ship to get in to the Kahiltna Glacier later this month. In certain ways it is better than a helicopter, as it is OK in soft snow and can land on quite a grade safely. It is incredible what a feeling of safety we get in Terry's little plane—a Piper Super Cub 150 with ski-wheels, able to land safely on either its wheels or its skis. The plane has a propeller that's slightly longer than usual for better performance at high altitude. When we took off from the Peters Glacier, despite an uphill run, we were in the air in slightly over a hundred yards.

When we got over the Muddy River, Terry impulsively decided to show me how small a gravel bar his plane could land on, much to my dismay. As we

Pilot Terry Moore checks the ski wheels on his Super Cub airplane. Using a hydraulic device in the cockpit, Moore could speedily pump the skis up or down, so the airplane could be operated either off a runway or a glacier.

landed I felt a funny little jerk, and when we got out we were horrified to see that we'd hit an old stump and torn off our entire right horizontal stabilizer.

Just as I got out of the plane, I sighted a huge Toklat grizzly bear about a hundred yards from us, heading our way. We had no gun and it looked for a few minutes as if our misery would be compounded by having a bear tear the plane apart. But to our amazement, he stopped a few yards away, lay down in the gravel, and watched as we worked on the plane.

In my rucksack I always carried a few emergency tools and supplies: a couple rolls of adhesive tape, a spool of copper wire, a Swiss scout-knife, and a pair of pliers. We cut down a small bush and used it as a splint to strengthen the torn aluminum in the stabilizer. Then we tied the bent aluminum with the wire and patched the torn fabric with lots of adhesive tape. As we worked, the bored bear finally got up and slowly walked away. In less than an hour, we were on our way again, headed for Fairbanks.

SUNDAY, JUNE 3

Cloudy and rainy all day. But Terry was determined to do a bit more exploration of the wilderness at the end of the Kahiltna Glacier. So we flew over Broad Pass and down the Chulitna Valley again to get to the Kahiltna area. How terribly rugged that country must have been for the early explorers.

We finally flew past the end of the glacier and landed at the tiny Chelatna Lake airfield. We didn't know that there was a landing spot in that region, and we're delighted to have a good little bush airport exactly where we might soon need one. The rain stopped and we decided to fly on to Anchorage, where we are now spending the night.

MONDAY, JUNE 4

Anchorage. Rain and low clouds all day. Jim Gale and I went to Elmendorf Air Force Base and checked our plans with the commanding general. Jim is the top sergeant of the Emergency Rescue Squadron here, and he knows exactly how to get things done. All OK for good cooperation with our McKinley expedition.

THURSDAY, JUNE 7

Turned forty-one years old today. Flew to Talkeetna, where the local railroad section foreman loaned me six men for an hour to clear the trees and brush away from the USGS Talkeetna survey station, which will be important to our mapping later on.

I'm staying at the Fairview Inn in Talkeetna tonight. McKinley is just sixty miles from here and can be seen right out the window in good weather. To bed at 7:45 for a real night's sleep. The weather looks genuinely rotten. Terry has flown back to Fairbanks in disgust. The most uneventful birthday I've ever had.

TUESDAY, JUNE 12

Decided it was worthwhile to investigate the Kahiltna Glacier for possible safe landings on the bare ice, using Don Sheldon's Super Cub, which has special four-wheel landing gear. It was a two-hour flight with completely unsatisfactory results. There was nothing wrong with the landing gear, but the ice on the lower part of the glacier is nothing but ruts and holes from healed crevasses. There is no place on the Kahiltna where anyone would want to try a wheel landing except in a real emergency.

We flew clear up the glacier to the upper end of the great 6,200-foot plateau about abreast of Mount Hunter. There one could land anything on skis. There are at least five miles of absolutely smooth, level snow with no crevasses or even bumps.

Later I took the train four-and-a-half hours to Anchorage and met up with Jim Gale, Henry Buchtel, Bill Hackett, and Barry Bishop. All of the food and other supplies are here. We plan to get rolling in a very few days.

SUNDAY, JUNE 17

Up at 2:30 a.m. to fly in a Cessna from Anchorage to thoroughly reconnoitre our proposed landing area way up on the Kahiltna Glacier. No luck—drizzle, southwest wind, and black clouds above the 3,000-foot level on the glacier. New snow everywhere, but the weather does seem to be mending ever so slowly.

Terry Moore is now back in Anchorage, and he plans to stay with us until we're landed on the Kahiltna. John Ambler, Mel Griffiths, and Jerry More arrived this morning from Denver, and at last our entire party is in Alaska.

The battle plan is for four of the men—John, Mel, Jerry, and Barry—to travel by train to Wonder Lake, 35 miles to the north of Mount McKinley. From there they will come in to the mountain by pack train in order to study the geology of the north side of McKinley on the way. The rest of us—Jim, Bill, Henry, and I—will fly in directly to the Kahiltna Glacier, as high as possible, then climb up the glacier to the pass at its head and establish an advance base camp. Our entire team of eight men will reunite there.

ON THE KAHILTNA GLACIER (7,600 FEET)
MONDAY, JUNE 18, 1951

We're on the way!

Henry Buchtel and I are now safely camped at 7,600 feet, above the last icefall on the Kahiltna Glacier—exactly where we wanted to be. We're only about four miles below Kahiltna Pass. It is totally calm here, so quiet that you can hear your own heart beat when the stove is turned off.

We are in our little 7-by-7-foot Logan tent, supper just finished, and ready for bed. The cloud tops are only just above us and we can get glimpses of Mount Foraker, all pink with alpine glow. My what a good feeling it is to be here after all these months of hoping and planning.

I took off from Anchorage at 2:15 this afternoon and flew to Chelatna Lake in a Cessna seaplane. Henry Buchtel followed in a second Cessna, and then Terry came in with his little Super Cub on ski-wheels. We were all just plain sick of Anchorage dust and high prices and glad to be at Chelatna. We had every bit of our stuff and we were eager for action.

A couple of violent little rain squalls blew by at the lake, but Terry and I decided that we'd take a try for a Kahiltna Glacier landing, just on the chance of a local opening. So we changed into our winter underwear right on the spot, there being no girls within forty miles in any direction.

Gorgeous weather with endless mountain views greeted the climbers on this day at the Kahiltna Glacier base camp at 7,600 feet.

We loaded the Cub with the basic gear for our camp. At exactly 5:00 p.m., Terry and I climbed in and we were off—not actually expecting to go very far, but ready to establish a beachhead on the glacier if we had the slightest chance to do it.

There was no blue sky anywhere, and dark clouds hung around the peaks. We swung up the lower rock-covered part of the Kahiltna Glacier. You couldn't even land a helicopter in those God-forsaken piles of rock-covered ice; some of the boulders are as big as bungalows. As we turned the fog-draped corner, we caught a glimpse of the icy peak of Hunter soaring far up into the clear blue sky above a 14,000-foot sea of fog.

We pressed ahead to our proposed landing area above the last icefall of the Kahiltna, and right at the base of McKinley. We skimmed over the lower part of the glacier—huge, yawning crevasses below us as we crossed the crest of the icefall.

There was no sun on the area where we wanted to land, making it about impossible to estimate our altitude in the grey nothingness that surrounded that spot. So we flew back down the glacier for a couple of miles and lazily circled there for a while, taking a look at our campsite every few minutes. At exactly 6:00 p.m., a thin streak of sun hit the spot, providing shadows and some visual perspective for our landing. We pounced on the opportunity, landing immediately and perfectly, not even a bounce.

With the weather so unpredictable, Terry didn't stay long with me. After unloading all my stuff, the two of us had quite a time getting the plane turned around for takeoff, as the slush was very deep and the crust on top not even thick enough to support a footstep. But Terry managed to take off down the 15 percent grade without the slightest trouble. The sound of his plane soon died out and I was left alone in the midst of a pile of stuff that would soon become our base camp.

An hour of work in the lonely silence of the vast, fog-draped basin and I had a flat platform stamped out and the Logan tent up and ready for occupancy. Sitting beside my radio, I brewed a bit of tea, a drizzle of snow pattering gently on the roof.

At 8:15 p.m. Terry called me on his radio, reporting his position five miles north of Chelatna Lake, headed for my camp with Henry Buchtel aboard. At 8:45 p.m. he radioed again, asking if I could hear or see him: "I am flying through very milky conditions [snow drizzle] about five miles below your camp. I haven't heard you and can't see you."

I went outside and at once spotted him and heard the distinct, lovely hum of his plane. My, what a tiny little lonely mosquito that plane was in the vast Kahiltna amphitheater!

I quickly radioed to Terry: "Conditions here marginal; local ceiling 300–500 feet; absolutely calm. I've marked the beginning of a 400-foot runway with snowshoes and a duffel bag to help your depth perception. I'll stand at the upper end of it near the tent."

Terry circled my camp once and then cut his motor as he banked over toward the fog-hidden mass of Mount Hunter. At 8:50 p.m. he made a very nice landing, considering the abominable conditions—just one bounce.

The clouds were closing in above. Foraker was gone for good and the Kahiltna Peaks were rapidly vanishing as Terry, Henry, and I emptied the plane of its load and turned it around. Terry speeded on his way again at 9:04 p.m. Now there were two of us on the vast Kahiltna Glacier.

TUESDAY, JUNE 19

The weather has taken a decided turn for the worse. After a bit of supper, Henry and I roped up and made a little trip up the glacier on snowshoes. It felt as if we were trudging in the air, as everything was white. We marked our trail at frequent intervals with tiny birch dowels, each three feet long and three-eighths of an inch thick, painted jet-black on the upper end. We had hundreds of these trail markers with the expedition and used them constantly to indicate our route up McKinley. (But we continued to call them "willow wands," because Alaskan climbers formerly used willow trail markers.)

Later it began clearing and we took another trip up-glacier. We went almost halfway from our camp to Kahiltna Pass, a good two miles, to an altitude of about 8,300 feet and left a bundle of sixty willow wands. We got

Terry Moore poses with his airplane on June 25, 1951, after setting a record for the highest aircraft landing ever in Alaska—10,000 feet, just below Kahiltna Pass on the Kahiltna Glacier.

our first awe-inspiring views of McKinley, Hunter, and Foraker as the mists slowly melted away.

WEDNESDAY, JUNE 20

Henry and I trudged up to within a few yards of 10,300-foot Kahiltna Pass, very near to where we plan to establish Advance Base Camp. It was an eight-mile round-trip. We both left our forty-pound loads at the beginning of the steep final slope, as the going was very hard in loose snow with breakable crust. We've now got an excellent trail, marked all the way with willow wands.

Terry Moore made an unannounced landing in the early evening with Bill Hackett. Then he turned right around, flew back to Chelatna, picked up Jim Gale and brought him on to camp with all the rest of our gear. Both landings were made under terrible conditions, with light snow falling.

The hum of Terry's plane has died away in the fog and at last all four of us are on the Kahiltna and ready to go. Let's hope for a spell of really good weather.

THURSDAY, JUNE 21

Betsy's birthday today. It's hard to believe that our youngest child is now five years old.

Clear and hot this morning. The highest temperature has been only 38, but it seems like 90. Terry Moore, God bless him, landed twice at our 7,600-foot camp and then relayed two huge loads of our stuff a mile and a quarter up the glacier and dumped them at an elevation of at least 8,000 feet. He doesn't yet want to attempt a landing at our Advance Base Camp at 10,000 feet, near Kahiltna Pass, as the temperature is so hot that the snow is too sticky for a takeoff. He's eager to try it as soon as conditions improve.

At the 8,000-foot site, I am literally cowering from the heat, sitting on a packboard with my light, white shirt pulled over my head. We set the tent up at the very apex of this magnificent amphitheater and decided to stay in it until the temperature cools off in the evening before trekking upward.

After supper we made a long, tough climb to Advance Base Camp at 10,000 feet. We hauled some big loads up here using snowshoes all the way.

We had to dig down through about thirty inches of snow before we could find a good firm base for the tent. We didn't make it to bed until 12:30. Four men in one tent is a real jam, along with radio and all cooking gear. The Air Force in Anchorage has told us that if the weather holds, they'll make a major airdrop of our stuff here at 9:00 a.m. tomorrow.

ADVANCE BASE CAMP BY KAHILTNA PASS (10,000 FEET)

FRIDAY, JUNE 22, 1951

At 6:30 a.m. the Air Force C-47 appeared, and before we could even get out of our tent, they started dropping supplies all over the place. They made at least a dozen passes at extremely low altitude and heaved out more than a ton of stuff, in forty-three pieces. Five of them came down under parachutes, but the rest were free-fall.

Included in this shower of equipment was a small L.L. Bean sled. We spent the afternoon collecting the stuff and sledding it into camp. We also stamped out a long landing field, thirty feet wide, for Terry's plane. It was a real scorcher of a day.

This is certainly a magnificent spot. One good feature of this location is that the sun doesn't hit the tent until nearly 7:00 a.m. and it's easy to sleep late.

After an early supper, the weather suddenly changed. A stiff, 20-mph breeze brought with it an inky pall of clouds that blocked the valley to the south. We redoubled our efforts to complete making our camp. We got another seven-by-seven Logan tent up before supper. After supper we set up an eight-by-ten wall tent with five-foot walls and an eight-foot ceiling—all airdropped to us today. We have everything stored neatly away, and our frozen food is in a deep underground cache.

With all of the equipment now in hand, it reminds me that we're not just trying to find a new route up Mount McKinley. We're also about to begin precise survey observations to add to the work that we did when we were on this mountain in 1947. We hope that eventually our work will produce a beautiful and accurate map of this great peak and its surroundings.

Bill Hackett cautiously probes a small cornice marking the 10,300-foot crest of Kahiltna Pass. The surface of Peters Basin lies in the lower right corner, 2,000 feet below.

Brad Washburn's survey crew climbs from their 10,000-foot Advance Base Camp up the steep slope of 12,525-foot Kahiltna Dome, the most important surveying station on the west side of Mount McKinley.

The West Buttress of Mount McKinley towers 3,000 rocky feet above the expedition's 13,000-foot camp at Windy Corner.

Expedition members pack heavy loads across the 14,000-foot plateau of the West Buttress route. Lofty 17,400-foot Mount Foraker towers above the climbers toward the southwest.

Most members of the party wore bearpaw snowshoes up to the 15,500-foot camp, just at the foot of the steep slopes leading to the top of the West Buttress.

waterproofed. But it is all iced up, particularly the door, which is almost impossible to shut. The storm has abated a bit. But just as I wrote that sentence, a big gust hit at 80 mph. We have a good anemometer here and the wind speeds that we're recording are really accurate. We are certainly wise to have named this spot Windy Corner!

The fellows down at Kahiltna Pass report a temperature of 31 degrees. They've had intermittent snow and rain all day, a miserable, slushy mess. So I guess everyone has had a rough day of it.

FRIDAY, JULY 6

Big blow all last night, but warm and cozy in the igloo. When I got up at 7:30, the tunnel was all blocked again with drifted snow and the tent half-buried.

The weather on McKinley is different everywhere. There is lovely sunshine out now and the wind is blowing no more than 35. There's blue sky overhead, and a superb sea of clouds 2,500 feet below us. At the same time there is a terrific gale aloft and an evil cirrus plume covering McKinley's summit. Weather reports presage more wind and trouble.

We took a load up to 14,000 feet this morning—to the end of our trail of six days ago. The wind started again, and our plans for building an igloo there were quickly wrecked. The loose snow is so deep that we've decided not to camp there at all and have returned to Windy Corner in disgust.

It's been a lovely afternoon, but now a curtain of clouds has rolled in, and a new plume has appeared over McKinley's summit. The sunset to the south was as beautiful as that to the west was disturbing.

BERGSCHRUND CAMP (15,500 FEET)
SATURDAY, JULY 7, 1951

We left Windy Corner at 9:00 a.m., making a foray to mark the trail onward toward Denali Pass. The weather was perfect except for the usual high winds aloft. Jim, Bill, and I made the 14,000-foot cache in an hour and then tackled the steep slope up onto the West Buttress with rough-locked snowshoes.

(For "rough-locking," we weave some cord back and forth in the web of the snowshoes so they don't slip backward while climbing a steep slope.)

The snow was abominable: deep and loose, with layers of thin crust that would support us only if we were wearing snowshoes. We finally wound up just plain shoveling a trail for the last two hours until we staggered, hot and exhausted, into the shelter of a big crevasse at 15,500 feet. This crevasse was a bergschrund, the place where the moving, lower slope of the glacier pulls away from the icy upper slope that is frozen tightly to the rock.

The others relayed supplies all day, making two trips up to 15,500. Jim and I got out the stove and cooked a little tea. We were sure that we could never make the 16,000-foot shoulder of the West Buttress today.

But after resting, we tackled the slopes above. Jim and I chopped steps steadily until 7:00 p.m. in the most wretched snow imaginable. There was crust on top. Then it was granular snow for a few inches. Then two thin layers of blue ice with powder between. It took us twenty to thirty chops per step.

As Jim and I neared the crest of the West Buttress at 16,000 feet, we moved gently to the right onto solid, steep rock, and at 7:15 we actually got slightly above 16,000. We had surmounted the crest, and the ridge that now rose above us for about a thousand feet looked like steep but easy scrambling.

To make the icy slope beneath us safer, we drove two big, wooden pickets into the crest where we stood, then unrolled about 600 feet of hand line all the way back down to the bergschrund. From now on, that miserable slope would be no less steep, but ready for safe climbing, both up and down. Then we retreated to a small but cozy igloo that Bill had made in the bergschrund while we were climbing above him.

We're making headway, but it's slow and tough.

SUNDAY, JULY 8

Got up at 8:30 at Bergschrund Camp after a good sleep. Cold only on the rear end! We are preparing for a reconnaissance to get as high as we can this afternoon.

Climbers got a stunning vista from the 15,500-foot camp, nestled in the bergschrund (crevasse) at the bottom of the route that led upward to the 16,000-foot crest of the West Buttress. Mount Foraker dominates this view beneath lenticular high-wind clouds to the southwest.

At an elevation of 16,000 feet, Jim Gale and Bill Hackett start up the steep, rocky ridge leading to the final campsite at 17,200 feet. Brad, as usual, lags behind to take more photographs.

Jim, Bill, and I headed up the fixed ropes at noon. On the way, we added some pickets here and there to straighten and solidify our fixed ropes, then had a late, hot lunch at 16,000 feet. My, but this is a magnificently spectacular route. The views of the Kahiltna Glacier, of Mount Foraker and Mount Hunter, are stunning in every conceivable combination of light and shadow.

The climbing between 16,000 feet and 17,200 feet is the oft-discussed key to this climb. We did it with heavy packs in exactly an hour and forty minutes, scrambling on firm rock and snow, well-packed by the wind. No technical problems at all.

It's so clear now that we can even see the hills behind Anchorage. There are broken clouds above us at about 20,000 feet, tearing along at at least 70 mph.

As we crested the ridge at about 17,200 feet, for the first time we had a look at Denali Pass, now only a thousand feet above us. It's temptingly close, the inky black cliffs of the North Peak towering behind it. We dumped our packs in a slight hollow behind the crest of the ridge, then hustled back down to our camp in the bergschrund—on the way getting some geologic specimens of the amazing contact zone between the McKinley granite and the North Peak argillite.

It's been a thrilling day. I wonder where we'll be tomorrow night?

HIGH CAMP (17,200 FEET)
MONDAY, JULY 9, 1951

We are now camped under gorgeous blue skies above a silvery sea of clouds, in the snow basin right below Denali Pass. This morning we got up at 6:30 back at Bergschrund Camp, in dense fog. Jim, Bill, and I had a quick breakfast in our little igloo and then speedily climbed up that icy, roped hillside with our final, heavy packs. We climbed back to the crest of the ridge and then dropped a trifle down the other side to this new camp.

Denali Pass, a thousand feet above us, seems a stone's throw away. Our objective is very nearly won. We're due for a few chilly nights, though. It's mighty cold, as we abandoned half of our sleeping bags down below to cut weight.

Large, warm over-mittens were worn over smaller regular mittens above 17,000 feet.

Jim Gale looks at Mount Foraker while at 17,250 feet on Mount McKinley. This ledge was close to the big igloo built by team members for shelter at their highest camp on McKinley.

Jim Gale (right) and Bill Hackett make their way up toward the crest of the West Buttress, the route protected by a fixed rope. Mount Foraker is in the background.

Summit of
Mt. McKinley
20,320

Harper Glacier

Denali Pass
18,200

High Camp of
West Buttress
Route 17,200

The final 3,000 feet of elevation gain via the West Buttress route began at the final camp at 17,200 feet, continued up to Denali Pass, and traversed over to the summit.

On July 10, 1951, Brad Washburn, Jim Gale, and Bill Hackett headed up the steep slopes leading toward 18,200-foot Denali Pass and their goal of accomplishing the first climb of Mount McKinley's West Buttress route. Here, Gale and Hackett were only 400 feet below the pass—and from there, they faced the final 2,000 feet of elevation gain to the summit.

This morning before leaving camp we put on our comfortable felt boots for the first time, and they have been a godsend. Up till now we've worn excellent rubber Mishawaka Thermopacks all the way. We had a breather and a thermos of hot tea at the top of the fixed ropes, then continued through dense clouds all the way to our 17,200-foot cache of yesterday afternoon. We couldn't even see a hundred feet ahead of us there. Willow wands led us instantly to our cache.

We reached our present campsite at exactly three o'clock, just as the clouds were breaking up. From four o'clock on, we've had a glorious clear, calm, warm afternoon.

We worked like hell for three hours building a huge igloo. For supper we had Lipton soup, frozen hamburger, fresh peas, minute potatoes, bread, butter, and fresh strawberries. After this gorgeous meal we went back outside to build an entrance tunnel and pile lots of snow onto the igloo's windward side.

The sun has just set behind the western spur of McKinley's North Peak. The clouds are gone. The lakes and rivers to the northwest are all gold. There is a new moon to the west of Foraker. My, what a sight. This route is not only the shortest and easiest on McKinley, but also the most beautiful.

Tuesday, July 10

Up at 8:00 a.m. after a warm night in only the inner linings of our sleeping bags. The temperature outside was about 3 degrees Fahrenheit, but in the cozy igloo it barely got down to freezing. After breakfast we planned to try to work out and mark a route to Denali Pass. It is a very steep sidehill and looked pretty icy in spots, but we'd make it if the weather gave us a break.

It was wonderfully clear and calm and we decided to take a crack at both Denali Pass and the summit of McKinley if the weather held. Jim, Bill, and I left camp at 10:20 a.m. equipped for anything. It was 20 degrees and no wind as we tackled the steep western slope of Denali Pass. This was the last unknown section of our new route up McKinley. In 1947 we had looked down this slope from Denali Pass, and we've always been sure that it would be a steep but speedy climb.

The sastrugi—the wavelike ridges of rock-hard, wind-blown snow often encountered on slopes like this—were enormous. The westerly winds must have howled across that bleak slope. The going was never really steep (the maximum was about a 40-degree angle) and the hard, icy snow alternated with breakable wind-crust over ice—essentially just what we expected. We took lots of pictures, moved slowly, and enjoyed ourselves a lot. And we reached Denali Pass at 12:15—in just two hours!

Reaching Denali Pass was the climax of this expedition: exactly what we had wanted to do. This route was now established as the shortest, safest, and easiest way to the top of Mount McKinley. We all shook hands joyously. Anything more that we did was pure frosting on the cake, as we now stood on ground well known to all three of us. Jim and Bill and I were all on the successful 1947 ascent of Mount McKinley, members of the summit party that also included my wife, Barbara—first woman to the top!

We stopped at the pass to examine the big cache of food and equipment that we'd left there four years ago. We found a ghastly mess. The yellow parachute that we'd left to cover our cache was in tatters and flapping in the wind, and a shovel was lying on the snow, a hundred yards east of the pass. There was horrible confusion at the cache. A subsequent climbing party, wanting supplies, had apparently cut the parachute off the cache, taken what they needed, and then just left it open to the elements.

Wind-driven snow filled every nook and cranny of that carefully protected cache. Two sleeping bags were filled with snow, and one of our stoves was out in the open. The whole cache was a solid, immovable mass of material cemented together with ice and snow. What criminal negligence. We were lucky that we weren't in serious need of the gear.

We dug deep enough into the cache to see that some sugar and oatmeal were dry inside a five-gallon can. Then we walked to the thermometer cache and opened it to check the minimum-temperature thermometer, which would indicate the coldest reading for Denali Pass in the past four years. It read minus 59 degrees Fahrenheit—a frigid spot.

At the edge of the cache, Jim found a little dead bird, a redpoll. It must

Jim Gale leads Bill Hackett as they start the final quarter-mile to the summit cone of 20,320-foot Mount McKinley.

have been looking for food and froze to death, after being swept up to that great altitude by a gale.

At one o'clock the weather was steadily getting better, so we decided that we would make a try for the top. We had plenty of willow wands in hand, and at the very least we would get the trail well-marked for a good distance. There were big plumes of icy fog over both the North and South Peaks, but I figured that as the afternoon went on and it began to get colder, those clouds would slowly disappear. It helps to be an intimate friend of this dear old mountain.

As we climbed slowly up the ridge, to our amazement we ran into lots of our 1947 willow wands. They had all been broken off, though, flush with the icy surface of the snow. My guess is that they had become loaded with frost and that the added wind resistance had snapped them. We found these little relics at intervals all the way.

At 19,000 feet we went into the fog and the breeze got brisker. I climbed a little to the left of our old route, heading for the hollow between the 19,000-foot shoulder and the formation known as the Archdeacon's Tower. We made this first thousand feet in exactly an hour. Jim and Bill were having a bit of hard going with the altitude, so I took all the trail markers and my cameras and put them together in my pack. This was the only time I've ever seen Jim Gale really tired. Curiously enough, I've never felt better, and the forty-pound load including the cameras (a tiny C-3 Leica, a Bell & Howell 141-B 16mm movie camera, and a 4x5 Speed Graphic) seemed not to bother me a bit. I was having one of those really good days.

Our approach to the summit was made blind, using a detailed knowledge of the mountain and using willow wands that we stuck in the snow to literally survey us in a straight line across the huge, level snowfield between the Archdeacon's Tower and the final steep summit slope. I set the basic course, marking the way with the wands, then Jim and Bill would yell when I swung either way out of a straight line.

We stopped for a forty-minute lunch in the dense fog and warm sun before going up that final hillside. We then wallowed through knee-deep powder snow for fifteen minutes because we had left our snowshoes behind. The skies were clear everywhere but on the very top of McKinley. This made me sure that if we continued moving slowly ahead that it would all clear as soon as the air began to cool off around 4:30 or 5:00 p.m.

That was a good theory. At 4:30 we were toiling up the summit cone among huge sastrugi when it suddenly started to clear. As we reached the crest of the shoulder, it cleared completely and we could see the big bamboo pole that we'd left on the summit four years ago.

From here it was only a short climb to the top, so I unroped and Jim and Bill went ahead while I photographed them against a cloudless blue sky. As I worked my way up after them, the view to the south was staggering. A 10,000-foot wall dropped off to the Kahiltna Glacier where we had landed three weeks ago. The green of the Tokositna Valley was wonderful to see, creeping far up among the icy peaks. Mount Hunter, which had long dominated our view, now looked utterly insignificant.

I caught up with the others atop the last big hump on the ridge, a hundred yards short of the top. I was totally overcome with emotion when at 5:30 we reached the summit and the whole amazing panorama burst upon us.

Our stay on top was geared to the weather and photography. When we arrived, there was only a light breeze. The temperature was at about zero and there were only a few scattered clouds to the northwest. We set to work to make a good series of movies and stills of both the top and the view. It was very cold work for the hands.

Forty-five minutes went by all too fast, and then all three of us were ready to leave. The wind was coming up again, and there was no longer any warmth from the lowering sun. We were all beginning to shiver.

We hated to leave. The view was so marvelous in every direction: our old friend Mount Hayes, far to the east; the Coast Range behind Anchorage, at least 150 miles to the south; and scores of mountains, lakes, and rivers stretching to the western horizon. I remembered for a moment the wonderful remark by Robert Tatum, who stood on this spot with the first-ascent party on June 7, 1913: "It's like looking out the windows of heaven."

An endless vista of Alaskan mountains and sky opened up for the climbers on the summit as they looked southward down the full length of the Kahiltna Glacier.

Brad Washburn, Jim Gale, and Bill Hackett reached the summit at 5:30 p.m. on July 10, 1951, completing the first ascent of Mount McKinley via the West Buttress route—now the favored route for almost all climbers. Hackett, left, and Gale display the American flag.

Expedition leader Brad Washburn stands at the summit. The moment marked his third—and final—visit to the top of North America's highest peak.

At 6:15 we tied our old bit of orange bunting back to the top of the bamboo pole and bade farewell to the summit. This was surely my last visit to this place. Then we headed off down the ridge. Jim Gale and I both admitted later that tears had trickled down our cheeks as we left.

We got back to Denali Pass at 7:30 and rummaged among the remains of our cache for a few food items that we needed and then covered it up again. Then we continued our descent to High Camp, still a thousand feet below us. We'd left a hundred-foot fixed rope at the icy top of the slope heading down from the pass, but that was but a tiny fraction of the distance and we had to be very, very careful. It's awfully easy to catch a crampon on your pants when you're tired at the end of a joyous day.

At 8:45, weary but happy, we crawled into our spacious igloo. It took a few minutes for us to come out of a daze of weariness to realize that we had actually made the first ascent of Mount McKinley's West Buttress.

WEDNESDAY, JULY 11

Jim, Bill, and I had a long, long sleep and a delicious breakfast, as one always likes to have after a long, hard, successful day. We cleaned and arranged the igloo for its next occupants. We also left them a lot of leftover food and fuel, because in our wildest dreams we never thought we'd climb the last three thousand feet of McKinley almost instantly. At eleven o'clock we started a leisurely trip downward, unroped to 16,000 feet to make it easier to take good pictures. It was warm and pleasant in the sun; the snow was perfectly dry and hard underfoot, and there was not a bit of wind.

Far below on the 14,000-foot plateau we saw five little specks starting upward and knew that we'd later meet them around 15,000 feet. We moved very slowly and cautiously to 16,000 feet. We weren't eager at all to spoil a perfect climb with a foolish accident on the way down, and the loose, wobbly rocks and icy snow patches were a good setup for a slip.

We stopped at 16,000 for over an hour and actually melted water to make some hot Kool-Aid for lunch. You certainly get dehydrated rapidly at that height. On the way down the fixed ropes the sun and heat were terrific. Almost all of our old steps had been melted out by the sun.

We met Barry, John, and Henry at 15,500 feet and left them there at our igloo in the bergschrund as we continued down. Tomorrow night they should reach the big igloo up at High Camp below Denali Pass. Mel and Jerry were pretty tired and Jerry had been sick all night with indigestion, so they dumped their loads and returned to Windy Corner with us in the blistering sun. We stayed at the Windy Corner campsite for a huge supper, and to wait for the sun to get down so the slush on the route below would harden.

When Jim, Bill, and I left Windy Corner, the trail was frozen hard. The descent wasn't as pleasant as we had anticipated, because all three of us were burdened with big loads of the geologic specimens that Mel and Barry had been collecting. But the descent took place on a gorgeous evening, and as we staggered into the cool clouds, the icy cliffs to our left were all pink with the last sunset. At midnight we arrived back at our Advance Base Camp just below Kahiltna Pass, hale, hearty, and supremely happy.

ADVANCE BASE CAMP BY KAHILTNA PASS (10,000 FEET)

THURSDAY, JULY 12, 1951

The weather remains magnificent. We figure that Mel and Jerry climbed back to our Bergschrund Camp today, and that Barry, John, and Henry went on up to the High Camp igloo. If this incredibly clear weather holds, those three should hit the top tomorrow and the others on Saturday, two days from now. That igloo is acting like a nice little motel.

I was up at 8:00 a.m. and hard at work all day on our radio. We had hoped that the Air Force helicopter might take us out, but the word came back that we won't get it. The helicopter must be off doing other work.

I sent a message to Terry at the University of Alaska, asking if he could fly in tonight or tomorrow morning to pick us up. I hoped he could fly us to Kantishna, north of McKinley, so we could complete our survey work from

Gathered at the Kantishna airstrip after completing the McKinley climb are (from left) Jim Gale, Brad Washburn, pilot Terry Moore, and Bill Hackett. The West Buttress route was also completed on subsequent days by the other five members of the expedition: John Ambler, Barry Bishop, Henry Buchtel, Mel Griffiths, and Jerry More.

The huge bulk of Mount McKinley crowds the sky in this view from near Wonder Lake, about thirty miles north of the mountain.

Wonder Lake while this good weather holds. Let's hope he gets the message and can reach us by radio.

Three p.m. Hot as hell. Have been straightening out things and packing. Taking pictures of equipment. Cloudless, windless. Just received wire from Terry: "Will come this evening as soon as possible."

Nine-fifteen p.m. Terry just landed. He had a very ticklish landing at our 10,000-foot camp because of grey, twilight conditions, and he almost turned back. He plans to make one flight tonight and three more after daybreak. I will go on the first flight. The problem I've been weighing is whether it is best for the leader to go last, or to go first on the first and most dangerous flight. The first freight flight out of here is doubtless the most questionable. I'm going on it. Jim will be last, as he is my most reliable man, in case Terry has any trouble on the last flights.

Terry and I flew off Kahiltna Pass at 9:45 p.m. with about ninety pounds of freight. Bill and Jim had worried looks on their faces as they watched us start bumping down the hardened, crusty runway. Then the bumps got lighter and, as we neared the last marker flag, we were off and flying. As we turned, it was hard to see how Terry had ever landed in such awful visibility. The camp seemed to be floating in the midst of a sea of grey milk. The great pink peak of McKinley towered high, cloudless and aloof above us.

We circled twice, cleared Kahiltna Pass, and sped out across that huge gulf of Peters Glacier. The ravages of the last three hot days have been terrific. All of upper Peters Glacier is a sea of slush. You could not possibly land where Terry and I had landed so easily six weeks ago.

The sun was setting to the northwest and glittering gold on Lake Minchumina and that "land of a thousand lakes." The tension cleared and we chatted freely as Terry throttled back the engine and began the forty-mile glide to Kantishna. I'll never forget that green valley, particularly the marvelous sweet smell of flowers and grass and life as we came in for our landing after sunset. The whole air seemed so soft and fresh and delicious after the cold, dry, dead air of the mountain and its glaciers.

We landed at Kantishna at 10:15, hiked up to Bill Julian's little cabin, and tumbled instantly into bed. I borrowed Bill's alarm clock in order to wake Terry for his next flight back to Kahiltna Pass. We're both dog-tired, but the weather looks as if it's changing and we must get Bill and Jim out before the next storm descends on us.

FRIDAY, JULY 13

Friday, the 13th. What a date to choose for an air evacuation from Mount McKinley!

After Terry flew off, I snoozed for an hour, lying flat on my back on the gravel of the Kantishna landing strip. Terry returned at 3:55 a.m. with Bill and a big load of stuff. The weather was rapidly going to pot, so he hustled off again at 4:10.

We expected him back again by 5:30 with Jim and our last load of freight aboard. While we waited, we ate a huge breakfast of nine fried eggs and about two pounds of bacon. But Terry didn't return.

At 7:00 we bummed a ride up to Wonder Lake to resume surveying. But still no Terry. We began to get genuinely worried, but at 8:00 we finally heard the welcome hum of his engine and then saw him on his way back here. He had been caught in a violent snow squall at Kahiltna Pass for an hour and nearly didn't get away from there at all. But it cleared a bit and he and Jim were able to take off. The shuttle is now safely over—but not without plenty of anxiety on our part. We wonder about the four men still on the mountain, and if they made it to the summit before this change in the weather.

It was hazy, hot, and cloudy, so we got no survey work done at all. I flew to Fairbanks with Terry, but I plan to return to McKinley Park by train tomorrow. A shave and a haircut in Fairbanks cost $3.50! But I needed it.

SUNDAY, JULY 15

Bill and I returned to Wonder Lake to finish my survey work there and were very lucky. The telescope of my beloved Swiss T-3 theodolite instantly picked up our target on Peak Z after locating our huge igloo target. This successfully ties our new survey on the western side of McKinley to the major network that we want to establish here on the northern side. But we still have a lot more work to do both here and on the southeastern approaches to the mountain before the dream of a complete McKinley map is realized.

Terry Moore returned to Kantishna this evening, bringing John and Barry off McKinley in two successive flights. John, Barry, and Henry had reached the summit on Friday, July 13. Henry was still back at camp with Mel and Jerry, who got to the summit on Saturday.

Everyone made the top!

TUESDAY, JULY 17

Henry, Mel, and Jerry are still marooned at Kahiltna Pass by stormy weather.

FRIDAY, JULY 20

It's inky black again and the three men still at Kahiltna Pass report "worse wind and weather than ever." The forecast is for two more bad days.

SUNDAY, JULY 22

At 2:00 p.m. Terry took off from Minchumina and landed at Kahiltna Pass—only to be promptly clouded in. He finally got off at 8:50 through an almost solid sea of clouds and flew to Kantishna with Jerry More. That left Henry and Mel and a load of freight still to come out.

MONDAY, JULY 23

Terry flew up to Kahiltna Pass at dawn and managed to extricate Henry. Low clouds made the landing very difficult, so Terry decided to make only one more flight—to pick up Mel, but no more baggage. This is just what he did.

All's well that ends well. We are all safely off the mountain, and Mount McKinley's West Buttress has been climbed with total success.

INDEX

Aerial photography, 12–14, 30, 44, 47, 51, 60, 103

Aircraft: B-18, 104; C-47, 96; Fairchild FC-2W2, 49; Fokker Super Universal, 50, 85; Lockheed Electra (twin engine), 12; Lockheed Vega, 21–24, 45; Piper Super Cub 150, 91

Alaska Climbers Hall of Fame, 15–17

Ambler, John, 89, 92, 126

Archdeacon's Tower, 118

Bates, Robert H. (Bob), 14, 47, 49, 54, 56, 68, 85

Bates Lake, 60, 70, 81, 85

Beardsley, Hartness (Harty), 49, 50, 56, 68, 75–77, 81

Bishop, Barry, 89, 92, 126

Boston Museum of Science (New England Museum of Natural History), 7, 12

Browne, Belmore, 15, 89

Buchtel, Henry, 89, 92, 94, 126

Carpe, Allen, 11

Carter, Adams (Ad), 15, 21, 22, 24, 36–41, 41–42, 49, 50, 54, 69, 75–77, 81

Cook, Frederick, 15

Daiber, Ome, 49, 50, 54, 56, 85

Dow, Russell (Russ), 21, 24

Gale, James (Jim), 15, 89, 92, 108–122

Goldthwait, Richard (Dick), 19, 21, 22, 26, 30, 44–45

Grand Canyon, 14

Griffiths, Thomas Melvin (Mel), 89, 92, 126

Hackett, William D. (Bill), 89, 92, 108–122

Harper, Walter, 11, 17

Haydon, Jack, 49–50, 52, 56, 68, 85

Holcombe, Waldo (Wok), 21, 22, 24, 41, 41–42

Kahiltna Glacier, 94

Karstens, Harry, 89

Kellogg, Howard (Hal), 21, 22, 24, 36, 41

La Voy, Merl, 89

Lowell Glacier, 49, 50

Maps and mapmaking, 14–15, 44, 47, 55–56, 58, 65, 70, 73, 89, 92, 96, 100, 104, 125–126

Matterhorn, The, 11

McGonagall, Charlie, 89

Meyring, Gene, 21–24, 30, 44, 45

Mont Blanc, 11

Moore, Terris (Terry), 8, 14, 89–91, 94, 96, 100, 103–104, 125–126

More, Jerry, 89, 92, 126

Mount Alderstone, 47

Mount Bertha, 14

Mount Crillon, 12, 19–45

Mount Dickey, 15

Mount Everest, 14

Mount Fairweather, 11, 19

Mount Hayes, 14

Mount Hubbard, 47

Mount Kennedy (East Hubbard), 47

Mount King George, 60

Mount Logan, 52, 60

Mount Lucania, 14, 47

Mount Marcus Baker, 14

Mount McKinley, 11–12, 12–14, 14–15, 87–126

Mount Queen Mary, 60

Mount Sanford, 14

Mount Steele, 14

Mount St. Elais, 52, 60

National Geographic Society, 12–14, 47–85

Nunatak Glacier, 75–77

Parker, Herschel, 89

Putnam, David (Dave), 21, 22, 24, 26, 44

Randall, Bob, 51, 52–54, 58, 60

Rasmuson Library, 8

Sled dogs, 52, 56, 58, 66, 68–69

South Crillon Glacier, 19

Stix, Robert (Bob), 21

Streeter, Edward (Ted), 21, 41

Stuck, Hudson (Archdeacon), 11, 15

Taylor, Andrew M. (Andy), 49–50, 54, 75–81

U.S. Air Force, 96, 104

U.S. Army, 14, 87

Washburn, A. Lincoln (no relation), 21, 22, 24

Washburn, Barbara, 8, 14, 15–17, 87, 116

Wasson, Everett, 49, 50, 85

West Buttress (Mount McKinley), 14–15, 87, 103–116

Woods, Henry S. (Bem), 21, 22, 24, 36, 41

PHOTOGRAPHY INDEX

Negative numbers for Bradford Washburn and Bradford Washburn/ National Geographic Society photographs:

Front cover   57-5728, 57-3947
back cover   86318, 86231
page 2   57-1917
page 6   5172
page 9   8110
page 10   3057
page 13   7407
page 16   3441

page 20   57-1888
page 21   57-1667
page 22   57-1729
page 23   57-2641
page 25   57-2675
page 27   57-1919
page 28   57-2823
page 31   57-1562
page 33   57-1852
page 35   57-1595
page 37   57-1605
page 38   57-2730
page 40   57-2802

page 43   57-2736
page 48   86432
page 51   86333
page 52   86425
page 53   not available
page 55   86220
page 57   86287
page 59   86232
page 60   86332
page 61   86318
page 62   86231
page 64   86218
page 65   not available

page 66   86162
page 67   86143
page 69   86066
page 71   2215
page 72   not available
page 74   not available
page 76   86119
page 78   86111
page 79   not available
page 80   86124
page 82   not available
page 83   86369
page 84   86341

page 88   57-5732
page 90   57-5758
page 93   57-5728
page 95   57-5765
page 97   57-5816
page 98   57-5851
page 99   57-5812
page 101   57-5859
page 102   7267
page 105   57-5871
page 106   57-5879
page 107   57-5776
page 109   57-5889

page 110   57-5897
page 111   57-5777
page 112   57-5904
page 113   57-5893
page 114   7302
page 115   57-5910
page 117   57-5926
page 119   57-5939
page 120   57-5929
page 121   57-5932
page 123   57-5942
page 124   3451

ABOUT LEW FREEDMAN

LEW FREEDMAN COVERS OUTDOOR ADVENTURES for the *Chicago Tribune.* Previously, he served for seventeen years as sports editor of the *Anchorage Daily News.* Author of more than a dozen books about Alaska, Freedman has worked frequently on stories with Barbara and Brad Washburn over the past decade.

Freedman has won numerous journalism awards in a career that has included work at newspapers in Pennsylvania, Florida, New York, and Alaska. A graduate of Boston University, he earned a master's degree from Alaska Pacific University.

Freedman and his wife, Donna, have a daughter, Abby.

ABOUT BRADFORD WASHBURN

DR. BRADFORD WASHBURN HAS MANY TITLES: Mountaineer, Explorer, Photographer, Mapmaker, National Geographic icon, Living Legend. He prefers to be known, with his wife Barbara, as the two people who built Boston's Museum of Science. Together they raised more than $200 million for the museum between 1939 and 1980.

As an explorer, Washburn got an early start, climbing his first mountain and publishing his first article by age 15. By the time he graduated from Harvard College in 1933, he already had established himself as an unusually competent expeditionary mountaineer, with four seasons of climbing in the French Alps and three expeditions to Alaska under his belt, including more than a half-dozen first ascents. Washburn has received countless awards worldwide honoring his achievements.

His wife of 60 years, Barbara Washburn, has received much acclaim for her part in many of his later explorations. Bradford Washburn often has been quoted, "Barbara is the most important event of my life." The couple lives in Lexington, Massachusetts.